Swords
&
Whetstones

Swords & Whetstones

A Guide to Christian Bible Study Resources

by Joe Allison

JORDAN*publishing*

An Imprint Of
EVANGEL PUBLISHING HOUSE
NAPPANEE, INDIANA

Jordan Publishing is an imprint of
Evangel Publishing House
2000 Evangel Way, P.O. Box 189
Nappanee IN 46550-0189
Toll-free ordering: (800) 253-9315
Internet Website: http://www.evangelpublishing.com

Cover design by George Foster, Foster & Foster Graphics

Publisher's Cataloging in Publication
(Provided by Quality Books, Inc.)

Allison, Joseph D.
    Swords & whetstones : a guide to Christian Bible
study resources / by Joe Allison. — 3rd ed.
    p. cm.
    Includes bibliographical references and index.
    Previous editions published as The Bible study
resource guide.
    LCCN: 99-90609
    ISBN: 1-891314-01-7
    1. Bible—Study and teaching—Bibliography. 2. Bible—Bibliography.
3. Bible—Study and teaching. I. Title.

Z7770.A45 1999   016.22
                                                          QBI99-852

Printed in the United States of America.
99 00 01 02 03 04 05 / 10 9 8 7 6 5 4 3 2 1

To My Wife

"Many a woman shows how capable she is,

but you surpass them all"

(Prov. 31:29, NEB)

Table of Contents

List of Figures

Preface

Welcome to an experiment. This is the second in a series of reference books which introduce the best printed Christian resources available today. The series differs from traditional reference books in three ways.

First, *these books are easy to comprehend.* Our editors have scaled them to a ninth-grade reading level. This makes them ideal reference books for people who do not have an advanced education. They're also helpful to readers who know English as a second language.

Second, these books differ from other reference books in their scope. *They are comprehensive at the same time they are easy to comprehend.*

"How's that possible?" you may ask. No book can give me every important fact on a given subject. Certainly, yours can't do that."

Indeed. Yet each of these books will give you a full orientation to the subject at hand. Each book will give you the most significant facts about the subject. And each book will give you the tools to find your way through the vast territory that is being opened to you. For these reasons, we call them comprehensive.

Third, *these books introduce you to the entire Christian world, not just one small region of it.* You'll find basic facts about Catholic, Orthodox, and Protestant resources here. We will invite you to appreciate and learn from the diversity of the Christian world.

Not everyone feels comfortable with this approach. Some readers entertain only authors who think as they do. They may in fact challenge the right of some authors to call themselves Christian. This is a legitimate concern.

How did we decide which authors' work to include in this "guide to Christian Bible study resources"? Who can rightfully claim to be "Christian"?

A Christian is a person in whom the Spirit of Jesus Christ lives. Christ informs a Christian's mind and guides a Christian's actions. His Spirit transforms a Christian's character so that the individual becomes like Christ, while still having his individual qualities (and flaws). This means we find a wide variety of people who are Christian.

At the same time, a Christian worships Jesus Christ and accepts His teaching as the Word of God. This means every Christian believes certain things in common with other Christians. Early Christians wrote several *creeds*[1] to help the rest of the world know what they believed. One of these statements, the Nicene Creed, is widely accepted by Christians today. (See p. xix.) These five short paragraphs tell us what Christians around the world have believed about Christ for nearly two thousand years. So we have used the Nicene Creed as a measuring stick to decide which books to include in this list of Christian resources. That simple decision drew together an amazing variety of things, as you will see.

You will find Catholic, Orthodox, and Protestant resources here. You will hear voices from liberal, conservative, and moderate wings of the Christian house. Charismatic and neo-Pentecostal believers will find their favorite authors here. So will those who come from liturgical churches, who may frown on charismatic experience. The Lord's house has many rooms indeed.

Of course, the Nicene standard of Christian belief excludes some books that you would otherwise expect to find here. For example, it excludes *New Age** books. New Age writers produce a marvelous variety of books on Scripture and spirituality. They also affirm most of Jesus' teachings. Yet they will tell you that they don't claim to be a Christian if it means ordering their lives around Jesus Christ—and it does.

We omitted some excellent books that a Christian might use for Bible study, because they are not Christian resources in themselves. An example would be the fine Jewish commentaries on the Old Testament.

Finally, we did not include the majority of good Christian books on Bible study, simply for the sake of space and economy. We would have amassed a directory several times the size of this one (and far more costly) if we had tried to include them all.

---

[1]Throughout this book, we have marked the first occurrence of technical terms with an asterisk (*) and defined them in the Glossary, pp. 187-97.

So if you feel offended by anything we have included or omitted, we beg your pardon. We think the experiment was worth that risk.

Earlier editions of this book appeared in 1982 and 1984 under the title, *Bible Study Resource Guide*. I wish to express my appreciation to the following persons, who helped to make each new edition of this book possible:

Robert Sanford and Ron Pitkin of Thomas Nelson Publishers; Al Bryant of Word, Inc.; and Mark Hunt of Zondervan Publishing House, who provided advance information about Bibles and reference books that were in process of publication.

Pauline Holsopple of Anchor Room Bookstore in Fort Wayne, Indiana, and the staff of the campus bookstore at Fort Wayne Bible College (now Taylor University's Fort Wayne campus), who loaned me review copies of new Bible reference books.

The library staffs of Concordia Theological Seminary of Fort Wayne, Vanderbilt Divinity School of Nashville, Aquinas College, and Calvin College of Grand Rapids, Michigan, who generously gave me access to their collections.

Sister Joyce Diltz and the religious community of the former Crosier Center of Fort Wayne, who gave me free access to their Roman Catholic reference library, along with several days of solitude for writing.

Ralph White of Logos Bookstores in Nashville, who reviewed major portions of each edition and made a number of helpful corrections.

Glen A. Pierce of Evangel Publishing House, for taking up the vision of this project and assuring that the new edition would be published.

My prayer partners M. Kay Colbert, Charles Harter, and Richard VanBeek, who have shared the burden of this book in prayer over the past seventeen years.

Joe Allison
Goshen, Indiana

Acknowledgments

The quotation on p. 51 is from *The History of the Scofield Reference Bible,* by Arno C. Gaebelein. Copyright © 1943 by Arno C. Gaebelein. Reprinted by permission of Loizeaux Brothers.

The first study Bible outline of the Book of Romans (top section of Figure 10, p. 62) is from *The Scofield Reference Bible.* Copyright © 1909, 1917, renewed 1937, 1945 by Oxford University Press. Reprinted by permission.

The second study Bible outline of the Book of Romans (bottom section of Figure 10, p.62) is from the *Spirit-Filled Life Bible.* Copyright © 1991 by Thomas Nelson, Inc. Used by permission.

The quotation on pp. 100-101 is from *The Living Talmud* by Judah Goldin. Copyright © 1957 by Judah Goldin. Reprinted by permission of New American Library.

The excerpt from the Bible dictionary entry "Jezreel" (p. 142) is from *The Zondervan Pictorial Bible Dictionary*, edited by Merrill C. Tenney. Copyright © 1963, 1964, 1967 by Zondervan. Used by permission.

The excerpt from the Bible encyclopedia entry, "Make-Up" (p. 143), is from *Eerdmans' Concise Bible Encyclopedia*, edited by Pat Alexander. Copyright © 1980 by William B. Eerdmans Publishing Company. Used by permission.

The quote from a Bible survey (pp. 165-166) is from *The Old Testament Speaks*, 3rd ed., by Samuel J. Schultz. Copyright © 1980 by Harper. Used by permission.

The quote from a Bible introduction (p. 166) is from *An Introduction to the Old Testament*, rev. ed. by Edward J. Young. Copyright © 1964 by William B. Eerdmans Publishing Company. Used by permission.

Scripture references noted "KJV" are from the *King James Version of the Bible*.

Scripture references noted "NAB" are from the *New American Bible*. Copyright © 1988 by the Confraternity of Christian Doctrine, Washington, D.C.

Special Features of This Guide

Terms that may not be familiar to the reader are printed in italics and marked with an asterisk the first time they appear. This marking indicates that the term is defined in the Glossary at the back of the book.

This guide occasionally refers to other Bible reference bibliographies that are no longer in print. These references are shown in parentheses as abbreviations with page numbers. The full publication information for these references is given below.

Bible Reference Bibliographies

BLBS—Wiersbe, Warren W., *A Basic Library for Bible Students* (Ada, MI: Baker Books, 1981).

BRW—*Recommending and Selling Biblical Reference Works: A Guide for Booksellers* (Grand Rapids: William B. Eerdmans Publishing Company, 1980).

CC—Spurgeon, Charles H., *Commenting and Commentaries* (Carlisle, PA: Banner of Truth, 1969).

GHR—Ramsey, George H., *Tools for Bible Study* (Anderson, IN: Warner Press, 1971).

HBE—Bruce, F.F., *History of the Bible in English*, 3rd ed. (New York: Oxford University Press, 1978).

HBS—Osborne, Grant R., and Stephen B. Woodward, *Handbook for Bible Study* (Ada, MI: Baker Books, 1979).

HSB—Job, John B., *How to Study the Bible* (Downers Grove, IL: InterVarsity, 1973).

ML—Barber, Cyril J., *The Minister's Library* (Ada, MI: Baker Books, 1974).

MTBS—Danker, Frederick W., *Multipurpose Tools for Bible Study*, 2nd ed. (St. Louis: Concordia, 1966).

PBS—Smith, Wilbur M., *Profitable Bible Study* (Boston: W. A. Wilde, 1951).

STB—Foster, Lewis, *Selecting a Translation of the Bible* (Cincinnati: Standard Publishing, 1978).

TBS—Kelly, Balmer H., and Donald G. Miller, *Tools for Bible Study* (Richmond, VA: John Knox, 1956).

English Bible Versions Cited in This Book

ASV—American Standard Version

KJV—King James Version

LB—Living Bible

NAB—New American Bible

NASB—New American Standard Bible

NEB—New English Bible

NIV—New International Version

NJB—New Jerusalem Bible

NKJV—New King James Version

NRSV—New Revised Standard Version

REB—Revised English Bible

RSV—Revised Standard Version

RV—Revised Version

TEV—Today's English Version

Introduction

Chuck came to me with a tough question. After serving as our church's youth advisors for several years, he and his wife had received a cash gift from the youth group and they wanted to buy some Bible reference books for their home library. "What should I buy first?" he asked.

Christians now have a wide assortment of Bible study aids available, and we thank God for that. But it's not easy to know which reference books are best suited to a particular person's needs. Chuck wanted to do more in-depth study of Bible theology, while his wife wanted some inspiring Bible-based devotional reading. What would help them accomplish both objectives?

I recommended that they start with *Strong's Exhaustive Concordance*, *Nave's Topical Bible*, and *Nelson's Illustrated Encyclopedia*. These three books would help them do lesson preparation, personal Bible study, and devotional reading. Chuck told me that they already had a copy of *Nave's Topical Bible*, so in its place I recommended the one-volume *Commentary on the Whole Bible,* by Jamieson, Fausset, and Brown.

Each Christian's Bible study needs are different. The reference books that I recommended to Chuck and Lucy would not be the best choices for a ministerial student who needs to study the ancient languages of the Bible. Nor would I recommend a Greek lexicon to a new Christian, who needs to undertake a devotional Bible study in the beginning stages of discipleship.

I have compiled *Swords & Whetstones* to help you decide for yourself which Bible-study aids are best for you. I have also provided information about the most popular English versions of the Bible, so you can choose a version for your personal Bible study. At the outset, however, I should mention some resources that you will *not* find here.

Swords & Whetstones does not include linguistic study aids or other reference books designed primarily for the graduate student. The goal is to survey the best printed resources for laypersons and pastors. While it's true that some people use lexicons, interlinear Bibles, and other sophisticated reference books in local parish ministry, that is quite rare. I believe that serious Bible students who are capable of using such tools will probably learn to use them in the graduate classroom; so it would be superfluous to give them instruction here.

Swords & Whetstones does not contain a chapter on computer software for personal Bible study, even though Christian publishers now offer a good variety of software products for this purpose. Software was omitted because the operating systems for personal computers are still changing rapidly, giving computer software a short life. Just five years ago, most Bible reference software was designed for Intel-based 386 IMB-PC systems. Then came the 486 and Pentium/MMX systems in rapid succession, each with a different operating platform. As a result, software that was then advertised as "state of the art" has now gone to the scrap heap.

The short obsolescence cycle will continue until computer manufacturers and software designers agree on more enduring standards. Until then, I suggest that you check with your local computer dealer for the "latest and best" Bible study software. Just be aware that today's Bible-study software may not work on the computer system you buy a couple of years from now.

The Internet offers you some excellent Bible study resources as well. Entire Bible versions, concordances, and other reference tools have appeared online in the past couple of years. I encourage you to be alert to the new opportunities in that venue.

Here I have tried to explain simply and clearly how you can use each major type of Bible reference book to enrich your personal study. Following each "how to" section is an annotated bibliography, to help you make your own comparisons and decide which study tool may be best for you. *Swords & Whetstones* does not include every Bible reference book that you may have heard mentioned, but you will find many of them here.

This guide invites you to keep coming back to the Word of God to learn more. "For the word of God is living and powerful, and sharper than any two-edged sword, piercing even to the division of soul and spirit, and of joints and marrow, and is a discerner of the thoughts and intentions of the heart" (Heb. 4:11-12). Here you will learn how to handle your spiritual "sword" and the tools to keep it sharp.

Joe Allison
Goshen, Indiana

The Nicene Creed

(This creed grew out of the Council of Nicea in A.D. 325. It took its present form sometime in the sixth century A.D.)

❖ I believe in one God, the Father Almighty, Maker of heaven and earth, and of all things visible and invisible.

❖ And in one Lord Jesus Christ, the only-begotten Son of God, begotten of the Father before all worlds; God of God, Light of Light, very God of very God; begotten, not made, being of one substance with the Father, by whom all things were made.

❖ Who, for us and for our salvation, came down from heaven and was incarnate by the Holy Spirit of the Virgin Mary, and was made man; and was crucified also for us under Pontius Pilate. He suffered and was buried, and the third day He rose again, according to the Scriptures; and ascended into heaven, and sits on the right hand of the Father; and He shall come again with glory to judge the living and the dead; Whose kingdom shall have no end.

❖ And I believe in the Holy Spirit, the Lord and Giver of life; Who proceeds from the Father and the Son[1]; Who with the Father and Son together is worshiped and glorified; Who spoke by the prophets.

❖ And I believe in one holy catholic and apostolic Church. I acknowledge one baptism for the remission of sins; and I look for the resurrection of the dead, and the life of the world to come. AMEN.

---

[1]Eastern Orthodox Christians omit the phrase, "and the Son."

Chapter One

Bible Study for Busy People

In April 1997, I conducted a survey of 220 Christian readers on the Internet. I wanted to find out how the electronic age had changed their book-reading habits. They still had a voracious appetite for knowledge. In fact, most of them had purchased six or more books in the preceding year, despite being enthusiastic "Web surfers."

I asked what types of books were hard to find. They said that wasn't a problem. Even an American missionary living in Kenya wrote, "We're just an hour's drive from Nairobi, so we can get any book that's in print." Others echoed his sentiment. They could find a book on any topic, by virtually any writer, at the stroke of a key. With the advent of online bookstores, they could have most books delivered to their doorstep within a day or so.

Instead these folks faced another problem. "We don't have time enough to read the books we have!" they said. A pastor in Michigan put it well: "I need help to sort through it all, so I can focus my attention on the information I really need."

Perhaps you feel the same way. We live in an age of "information overload." Tens of thousands of new books pour from the printing presses each year. Hundreds of thousands of pages of facts scroll across the computer screen. We don't need to find more information—we need to find the *right* information.

Yet we have less time to go digging for it. The demands of life increase daily. We pack our planning notebooks with "must do" tasks. The optimistic prediction we heard just a few years ago, about a shrinking work week and growing leisure time, has failed to materialize.

We are busy people—busier than ever.

And we are spiritually needy people—needier than ever.

How can we focus on the information we need to grow spiritually? Where can we find the insights we need to deal with the most crucial questions of life?

Some will say, "That's simple. Study the Bible." But the Bible is not a simple book. Even someone familiar with Scripture can be puzzled by the seemingly contradictory advice it gives. An understanding of the Bible comes with a careful, prayerful reading. That takes time. Christians want to spend their reading time effectively in Scripture. That won't just happen. We need help. We need tools that enable us to cut through the complexity of the Bible and lay bare its teachings that apply to our situation, here and now.

This book will help you get started. Think of it as your toolbox for Bible study. In *Swords & Whetstones*, you will find the right implements to get answers to your questions in Scripture. This resource won't take the place of diligent study, but it can make every hour of study time well-spent.

Meaningful Bible study begins with your desire to study the Bible and savor "the depths of the riches both of the wisdom and knowledge of God!" (Rom. 11:33, KJV). There's the key—desire. If you are truly hungry for the Word of God, nothing can keep you from studying it. If you are not hungry for the Word, pray that the Lord will whet your appetite for it. Then stimulate that desire by giving yourself a diet of Bible study that is *steady* and *satisfying*.

Steady Bible study is important. Some people read the Bible only when they "feel spiritual." Others read it only when they "need a lift." But read the Bible regularly—if possible, every day—and you will find God speaking to you, regardless of your mood. That will tantalize you to read His Word even more.

Satisfying Bible study (i.e., Bible study that meets your spiritual needs) is just as important. The more you have your questions answered, your dilemmas resolved, or your conflicts quieted through Bible study, the more you'll want to dig into this Book! The Holy Spirit does these things as we read. He reveals the truth of Scripture to us (John 16:13-14), just as Jesus revealed the truth of Scripture to His disciples (Luke 24:25-27, 32). The Holy Spirit brings us satisfying Bible study as we engage in steady Bible study.

We can facilitate the Spirit's work by the way we study. So proper Bible study methods are important. In the next few pages, I will describe three basic methods of Bible study. To make them easy to remember, I refer to them as three different kinds of "scopes" for looking into Scripture. There are many other methods, but these three will serve you well for most Bible study that you choose to do.[1]

A Periscope: The Devotional Method

Imagine you live on a submarine, traveling through hostile enemy waters. For days at a time, you don't come to the surface. You don't need to. You have the provisions to live underwater until it's safe to come up.

But now and then, you must get your bearings. You need to check some landmarks (perhaps even check the stars) to verify your position on the map. So you send up a periscope to peer around and get a fix on something that will confirm your location. Devotional Bible study is like that. It allows you to get a quick glimpse of the truth, in order to confirm your position. It can't reveal everything you need to know, but it reveals enough to keep you going!

When you hear a friend speak of having "daily devotions" or a "devotional study time," what image comes to your mind? Perhaps you picture someone sitting alone with an open Bible, reading a passage of Scripture and then spending a few moments in prayer. Yet the word *devotion* has a deeper meaning that may not be apparent from this image.

Devotion is a private act of worship. Our English word *devotion* comes from the Latin *devovere*, which means "to vow completely." So a time of "devotions" is a time to give ourselves completely to the Lord. We dismiss all thoughts about job, family, finances, or whatever else may have occupied our minds. We give our minds to the Lord. We release all anxiety, apprehension, resentment, or any other feeling that is alien to Christ, and give our emotions to Him.

We give even our bodies to Him. There are times when we must devote the body to some other task while we devote the mind to him; but in the time of devotions, we give the body to Him as well. We may kneel in prayer or sit in a relaxed position or raise our

---

[1]Howard F. Vos describes sixteen different methods in his fascinating book, *Effective Bible Study* (Grand Rapids: Zondervan, 1956).

hands, whatever position best expresses our full surrender to the Lord.[2]

The significance of this personal surrender becomes even clearer when we consider the corresponding Old Testament word, *cherem* ("devote" or "devoted"). When an Israelite chose an animal for sacrifice to the Lord, that animal was considered "a devoted thing." The Law forbade the worshiper from taking back the animal or using it for some other purpose (see Lev. 27:28-29). When he brought oil, wine, or grain to the temple as an offering, the goods were considered *cherem*, and he could not take them back or divert them for his own uses (see Num. 18:11-14). Anything devoted to God was abandoned to God; it was surrendered to God without any reservations or conditions.

So when we engage in "devotions" according to the biblical pattern, we surrender our entire selves to Him—body, mind, and all. This contradicts the notion that "devotional Bible study" is a casual, halfhearted affair. This method of Bible study requires no less effort than any other. In fact, it demands our complete attention.

Also notice that our English word *devotion* implies a "vow" or promise to God. You may promise God that you will worship Him at a given time (perhaps each day). If you promise to study His Word as part of that worship time, your promise makes it a devotional Bible study. You study God's Word to fulfill your promise to serve Him with this spiritual discipline.

Many Christians fail to continue devotional Bible study because they miss this point. They feel they need to know more of God's Word, so they promise themselves that they will study the Bible every day, every week, or whenever. In other words, they make a resolution. Now we all know what usually happens to resolutions: When we run into problems, we bargain with ourselves and change our resolve. When we make good progress, we congratulate ourselves by allowing "just one" indulgence; and before we know it, the resolution falls by the wayside. So it goes with those noble resolutions to study the Bible every day. It's too easy to excuse ourselves from self-imposed training.

---

[2]In Bible times, people often threw themselves headlong on the ground when they knew they were in God's presence (cf. Gen. 17:3; Lev. 9:24; Josh. 5:14; Matt. 17:6; and Luke 5:12).

But true devotional Bible study is not a resolution with ourselves; it is a vow to God. We don't do it to make ourselves more knowledgeable or more serene or more spiritual. We do it to worship God. So we do not govern the study by our feelings (e.g., "I'll not study the Bible today; I'm feeling blue"). Nor do we govern it by the change or lack of change we see in our lives (e.g., "I'll not study the Bible today; I'm not getting anything from it"). We study Scripture because we have promised the Lord we will do so.

The Bible encourages us to make such promises to Him. "Make vows to the Lord your God, and pay them," the Psalmist says (Ps. 76:11). Yet we are warned to take our vows seriously. "Better not to vow than to vow and not pay" the Preacher says (Eccl. 5:5). The writer of Proverbs advises that "it is a snare for a man to devote rashly something as holy, and afterward to reconsider his vows" (Prov. 20:25).

So devotional Bible study is not a casual or capricious thing if we follow the true sense of the word, *devotion*. If we read the Bible now and then, whenever the mood strikes us, in order to get some emotional "lift," then we might call it "occasional Bible reading." But we could hardly call it "study," and by no means should we call it "devotional Bible study."

So devotional Bible study (1) involves a complete surrender of ourselves, (2) fulfills a promise that we voluntarily make to God, and (3) honors or exalts the Lord.

Other Bible study methods are primarily for our own enrichment. They help us learn the content of the Word; they challenge us to grow according to the Word; they correct us in light of the Word. Such methods of study edify us and, as we are edified, God is glorified. But devotional Bible study reverses those priorities: Its primary purpose is to help us exalt or honor God. It induces a climate of worship; it gives shape and direction to our worship; it helps us respond to God and glorify Him. And as He is glorified, we are edified. With this purpose in mind, let me suggest these steps for devotional Bible study.[3]

---

[3]These steps follow the pattern suggested by J. Munro Gibson in *The Devotional Use of the Holy Scriptures* (London: National Council of Evangelical Free Churches, 1904), 46-52.

1. *Find a place of solitude.*

Solitude can be a Christian's friend. Solitude—that is, being remote or secluded from other people—can be the best environment for devotional study.

Many Christians think they must be completely cut off from the rest of the world for their devotional time, but that is seldom possible. The children are sleeping in the next room; the paperboy is wheeling past the window; rush-hour traffic rumbles in the background.

You probably will not have the solitariness that a monk or nun in a monastery cell might have, but you can have solitude. You can retreat temporarily from human contact and conversation to become more aware of God's presence. Even in the midst of David's tumultuous battles and victories, he sensed the Lord saying, "Be still, and know that I am God" (Ps. 46:10). David could not be alone, but he could be in solitude. So can you.

Go to a quiet room and close the door behind you. Turn off the radio, the TV, or the stereo. Block any other voices you may hear from the outside world. Unplug the telephone or take the receiver off the hook. If you are outside, find a secluded park bench or some other spot where people are not likely to pass by and strike up a conversation with you.

When you've achieved this physical solitude, move toward mental solitude as well. Don't concentrate on the dripping faucet, the airplane passing overhead, or any other distraction. Concentrate instead on the Lord. Ask Him to cleanse all other thoughts from your mind and all anxious feelings from your heart as you wait upon Him (Lam. 3:25-26).

2. *Realize the presence of the Lord.*

He is always near, but in the devotional time you will be more conscious of Him. You are not apt to see Him or hear His voice, but you can sense His presence with you as you can sense the presence of a friend beside you in a darkened room. As you put all distractions away, you will realize more vividly than ever how near God is to you. This is what James meant when he said, "Draw near to God and He will draw near to you" (James 4:8).

Even when you do not sense His presence, you can recognize His presence by faith. His Word says, "He who comes to God must believe that He is, and that He is a rewarder of those who diligently seek Him" (Heb. 11:6).

3. Read the Scripture.

Focus your thoughts on what the Lord clearly expresses in it. Avoid obscure or theologically complex Scriptures for devotional study. As Howard F. Vos advises, "The Bible student should avoid in his devotional life overemphasis on either extensive or intensive consideration of Scripture."[4] Remember, in devotional study you are not reading to gather new nuggets of information; you are reading to prepare for worship and to begin expressing your worship of the Lord. Read for the obvious (literal) meaning of the passage. What is the Lord plainly saying through these verses? What is the mood or tenor of the passage? Let your mind absorb the message and the mood. You will need a Bible version that is clear and easy to understand for this type of study. (See chapter 2.) Awkward or erudite phrases in some formal translations can distract you from devotional study.

For devotional purposes, some passages (such as the Psalms, the prayers, or the *doxologies** of the Bible) are more useful than others. So choose the Scripture passage wisely before you start. Figure 1 lists 100 Scripture portions well suited to devotional study. Use a topical Bible to locate an appropriate Scripture passage for worshipful study; for example, you may find helpful passages under topics such as "Prayer," "Praise," or "Adoration." In fact, if you use *Nave's Topical Bible* or some other that quotes most of the passages in full, you may read the passage itself from the topical Bible.

4. Consider what the Lord is saying to you at this moment.

Here you come to the crossing point between Scripture and your current life concerns. As you consciously wait in the presence of the Lord, let Him speak to you through His Word. This is the final step of self-surrender. Munro Gibson suggests that you ponder the following questions, along the lines of 2 Timothy 3:16:

> *Doctrine:* What may I learn of God? Of myself? Of the way of life? Reproof? Is there any sin of which I stand con-

---

[4]Vos, *Effective Bible Study*, 173.

Figure 1–Scripture Passages Recommended for Devotional Study

God's Attributes

Genesis 15:1
Genesis 28:10-16
Exodus 34:1-7
Deuteronomy 7:6-15
Deuteronomy 33:26-
  27
Job 5:8-26
Job 36:5-10
Psalm 32:6-7
Psalm 33:6-12, 18-22
Psalm 102:8-22
Psalm 121
Isaiah 6:1-8
Isaiah 9:6-7
Isaiah 33:16-24
Isaiah 40:10-26
Isaiah 57:15-21
Jeremiah 51:15-19
Lamentations 3:22-28
Ezekiel 34:11-17, 22-31
Amos 4:13
Nahum 1:1-13
John 1:1-13
John 3:16-21
John 8:12-29
John 10:26-30
John 14:5-14
Acts 17:24-31
Romans 5:1-2
Romans 8:32-39
Romans 11:33-36
1 Thessalonians 5:8-11
Revelation 4:8-11
Revelation 21:3-6

Doxologies, Hymns, and Songs

Exodus 15:1-18
1 Samuel 2:1-10
1 Chronicles 16:8-31
1 Chronicles 29:10-19
Psalm 8
Psalm 19
Psalm 29
Psalm 71:17-21
Psalm 77
Psalm 89
Psalm 146
Psalm 147
Psalm 148
Psalm 150
Isaiah 12:1-6
Isaiah 33:5-16
Isaiah 52:7-10
Luke 1:46-75
Luke 10:21-22
Ephesians 3:20-21
Philippians 2:5-11
1 Timothy 1:17
1 Peter 1:3-9
Jude 24-25
Revelation 1:4-6
Revelation 5:9-13
Revelation 7:9-12
Revelation 11:16-17
Revelation 19:5-7

Prayers

1 Kings 3:6-9
1 Kings 8:22-61
2 Kings 19:14-19
2 Chronicles 14:11

Nehemiah 8
Psalm 5
Psalm 51:1-17
Psalm 88:1-9
Psalm 90
Psalm 143
Isaiah 61:10-11
Isaiah 64
Jeremiah 32:17-27
Daniel 9:2-19
Matthew 6:9-13
John 17
Acts 4:23-30
Acts 20:32
Romans 15:5-6
1 Thessalonians 3:11-13
Hebrews 4:9-11
Hebrews 13:20-21
2 Peter 1:2-4

Exhortations

2 Chronicles 15:1-7
Isaiah 41:10-13
Matthew 5:3-12
Matthew 7:7-11
Luke 10:19-20
John 14:1-4
John 16:33
1 Timothy 6:13-16
James 4:7-10
1 Peter 5:6-11
2 Peter 3:11-18
1 John 3:1-3
1 John 5:7-12
Revelation 14:6-7

victed by the Word before me, which I must confess and forsake, and for which I must ask forgiveness?

Correction: Is there any wrong path I have been following, so that now I must change my course?

Instruction in Righteousness: What grace am I neglecting? And may I not be able now to add something to my life which will make it more harmonious and complete?[5]

Submitting yourself to the Lord's scrutiny is the climax of devotional Bible study. Aim to spend most of your study time at this stage. The Lord will reveal Himself as you ponder how His Word applies to you; it will be an experience that fills you with awe and adoration.

A commentary is not necessary for devotional study, not even one that is called a "devotional commentary." Your chief interest should be your personal encounter with the living Lord, so that you worship Him and yield yourself to His direction. Consulting a commentary may not move you any closer to this goal, and may in fact hinder you.

For similar reasons, I do not advise that you take notes during devotional study. Note-taking may cause you to analyze the text; it then becomes a mechanical task that takes the place of meditation and worship.

5. Close your devotional time with thanksgiving and praise.

Thank the Lord for His Word. Thank Him for the specific insights He has given you today. Praise Him for making Himself known to you.

A Telescope: The Deductive Method

When you are ready to delve deeper into the content of Scripture, consider reading an entire book of the Bible. This allows you to see the whole theme of a particular section of the Word. I

---

[5]The deductive method will not help you get a total picture of a Bible book that is actually a collection of heterogenous parts—a "mixed bag" of subjects. The Book of Psalms and the Book of Proverbs are examples; they are collections of many short writings, with no clearly logical or chronological order. These books are obviously not appropriate for deductive Bible study.

call this method of Bible a "telescope" because it allows you to step back from Scripture and get "the big picture."

Some writers call this the synthetic method, because it enables you to draw together the various elements of a Bible book to form one complete picture. (Our English word *synthesis* comes from the Greek *syntithenai*, which means "to place together.") Others call it the deductive method.

Regardless of what you call it, this method will give you a good grasp of almost any Bible book. You can also use this method to study a selected chapter, such as Romans 8 or 1 Corinthians 13, as long as the chapter deals with one central theme.

Get a looseleaf notebook to record your findings. Figure 2 shows how you might lay out two facing notebook pages for a given book. (I have shown the Book of Ruth as an example. This format works just as well with longer books such as Isaiah, although you won't be able to note as many details.) Here is a step-by-step method to use for the study:

1. Read the entire book once to get its basic theme.

Do this rapidly. Don't pause over interesting details, but skim-read the book to sense its overall thrust. Read it through in one sitting, so you are sure to get the full picture in mind at once.

(Many people shy away from deductive Bible study because they think it must take hours, but the books of the Bible are short. W.F. Crafts noted that 47 of these 66 books can be read in less than an hour, and you can read most of the New Testament books in twenty minutes or less.[6] So don't hesitate to try it.)

Remember, on this first reading you want simply to get the theme of the book: What is its chief message? What lesson of life does it illustrate? What warning or promise does it declare? When you have skimmed through the book once, you should know the answers to these questions. Write the theme in your own words on the appropriate line of your study notes.

On this first reading, you may also begin to get some idea of who wrote the book, who its first readers were, when it was written, and so on. If so, jot these things in your notebook as well.

---

[6]Cited by Frank T. Lee, *Bible Study Popularized* (Chicago: Winona Publishing Company, 1904), 107.

2. Read the entire book a second time.

Gather information about how and why the book was written. In other words, gather the information you need to fill in the rest of the first page shown in Figure 17 (p. 176). Here are some suggestions to help you find the information:

Writer: Usually, the writer will provide some sort of self-identification at the beginning or end of the book. (For example, Paul often mentions himself by name in the salutation of his letters.) The author's name also may appear in the title, such as "The Fifth Book of Moses, Called Deuteronomy" or, "The Epistle of Paul the Apostle to the Galatians." However, scribes assigned the titles of most Bible books long after they were first written. So when the title includes an author's name, don't assume it was placed there by the author. At best, the book's title gives you an early traditional understanding of who wrote the book.

In some cases, a Bible book does not identify its own author. Examples are the Book of Ruth and the Epistle to the Hebrews. When you encounter one of these books, note whatever clues you find about the author's identity. The Book of Ruth nowhere identifies its author, but you can pick up several clues: The writer was a historian (since this is a book of history), a genealogist (see Ruth 4:17-22), a person well acquainted with Hebrew marriage law (Ruth 3) and ancient Old Testament customs (Ruth 4:7-9). Beyond this, we are left to guess at the writer's identity.

Readers: Again, the book may indicate at its beginning or end who the intended readers were. This may be stated in the title (such as the "Second Epistle of Paul the Apostle to the Corinthians"—i.e., Christians at the city of Corinth). Even then, you may need to do some detective work to get this information. So it is with the Book of Ruth.

Time Written: When doing synthetic Bible study, you do not need to fix an exact date for the writing of the book; however, you should be able to tell the period of Bible history to which it belongs. For instance, you know the Book of Revelation was written in the New Testament age because it refers to Jesus Christ by name (Rev. 1:1), to seven "churches" in Asia (1:4), and to all Christians as "priests and kings" (1:6), a New Testament concept. You can perceive further that the book was written in a time of tribulation or persecution (see Rev. 1:9) and that it was written after

Figure 2–Deductive Bible Study Notes

DEDUCTIVE BIBLE STUDY NOTES

Book: Ruth   ○

Theme: a woman's loyalty

Writer: Historian   acquainted w/ OT laws
              Genealogist   & customs (chap. 3; 4:7-9)
                 (4:17-22)

Readers: Jews who lived in King David's time
                or later.

Period When Written: after the judges (1:1)   ○
                            after the sandal custom (4:7)
                            King David's time or later
                                (4:17-22)

The Writer's Purpose: To lift up Ruth as an
                             example to Jewish women.

                                                                           ○

Figure 2–Deductive Bible Study Notes (Continued)

DEDUCTIVE BIBLE STUDY NOTES

Rough Outline (List Major Ideas/Events):

○ Elimelech's family flees to Moab (1:1-5)
Elimelech's widow Naomi returns to Judah
(1:6-7)
Ruth returns with Naomi (1:8-22)
Ruth gleans in Boaz's field (Chap. 2)
Ruth offers herself to Boaz (Chap. 3)
Boaz takes Ruth as his wife (4:1-16)
Descendants of Ruth & Boaz (4:17-22)

○
Formal Outline (Organize Major Ideas/Events):

Intro. - Elimelech's family flees to Moab (1:1-5)
I. Ruth's loyalty to her mother-in-law
A. Elimelech's widow Naomi returns to
Judah (1:6-7)
B. Ruth returns w/ Naomi (1:8-22)
C. Ruth gleans in Boaz's field (Chap. 2)
II. Ruth's loyalty to her husband's family
A. Ruth offers herself to Boaz (Chap. 3)
B. Boaz takes Ruth as his wife (4:1-16)
○III. God rewards Ruth's loyalty
The descendants of Ruth & Boaz (4:17-22)

John was exiled to the island of Patmos (1:9). In a Bible dictionary's article on John or Patmos, you will find that this would have been late in the first century, probably under Emperor Domitian (reign A.D. 81-96). So the book was written not only to the seven churches of Asia, but also to other Christians who were being persecuted as John was.

The Book of Ruth poses a similar challenge when we try to identify its original readers. The book must have been written after the time of the judges, because it begins with the statement, "...in the days when the judges ruled" (1:1), phrased in the past tense. It must have been written after the Jews abandoned the custom of taking off a sandal to confirm a business deal, because it says "this was the custom in former times in Israel" (4:7). It must have been written in the time of King David or later, because the writer traces Ruth's family tree to David (4:17-22). All of this information tells us when the readers must have lived. Apparently they were Jews, because only Jews would have been interested in the Jewish king's ancestry. This process of discovery is one of the real joys of Bible study.

The writer's purpose: Sometimes the writer clearly states the purpose in writing a certain book, as when John says, "Jesus did many other signs in the presence of His disciples, which are not written in this book; but these are written that you may believe that Jesus is the Christ, the Son of God, and that believing you may have life in His name" (John 20:30-31). More often, you will have to discern the writer's purpose yourself. Ponder the theme of the book again. Was it written to encourage the readers? To warn them? To teach them? To accomplish something else?

The writer of Ruth may have had several purposes in mind. Perhaps the writer hoped to fill a historical gap in the Book of Judges; to explain how a non-Jew (Ruth) came to be a part of David's family line; or to record a romantic story from Israel's past. On the sample notebook page, I concluded that the theme of the book is, "A Woman's Loyalty." If this indeed was the writer's central idea, perhaps the book was written to present Ruth as an example to Jewish women, encouraging them to be loyal.[7]

---

[7]Some scholars feel the book may have been written after the Exile, in order to protest Ezra and Nehemiah's strict policy against having non-Jewish wives. I think this view is little more than a guess.

3. List the writer's major ideas.

This will require more careful reading than your first two times through the book, but it's still best to do this third reading in one sitting, in order to understand how one idea leads to another. Jot these ideas on the second note sheet, showing the chapter and verse for each idea.

Notice that you may need to do some further detective work in this phase of your study, too. The writer may openly state the idea that's being set forth, or the writer may simply illustrate the idea and you must discern what it is. The writer of Ruth uses the latter approach.

When reading a book of history, treat each event as an "idea" on your note sheet. Keep track of each major event you find, because the writer may use some of these events to illustrate a theme that he will set forth later.

4. Organize the major ideas into a formal outline.

An outline will help you see at a glance how the book is organized and how various parts of the book contribute to the entire theme. To make a logical outline, you must keep the theme clearly in mind as you consider each major idea of the book. Ask yourself how each idea relates to the theme. Is it a primary idea (one that declares the theme or some important aspect of it)? Or is it a secondary idea (one that explains or illustrates a less important facet of the theme)? In order to group the ideas of the book according to its major themes, you may need to reread portions of the book. Here is a list of ideas I gathered while reading the Book of Ruth:

Elimelech's family flees to Moab (1:1-5)

Elimelech's widow Naomi returns to Judah (1:6-7)

Ruth returns with Naomi (1:8-22)

Ruth gleans in Boaz's field (Chap. 2)

Ruth offers herself to Boaz (Chap. 3)

Boaz takes Ruth as his wife (4:1-16)

Descendants of Ruth and Boaz (4:17-22)

On my first pass through the book, I concluded that the overall theme of the book was, "A Woman's Loyalty." How do each of these ideas contribute to that theme? I have to do a little organizing of my notes, as follows:

The Book of Ruth:
"A Woman's Loyalty"
Intro.—Elimelech's Family Flees to Moab (1:1-5)
I. Ruth's Loyalty to Her Mother-in-Law
  A. Elimelech's Widow Naomi Returns to Judah (1:6-7)
  B. Ruth Returns with Naomi (1:8-22)
  C. Ruth Gleans in Boaz's Field (2)
II. Ruth's Loyalty to Her Husband's Family
  A. Ruth Offers Herself to Boaz (3)
  B. Boaz Takes Ruth As His Wife (4:1-16)
III. God Rewards Ruth's Loyalty
  The Descendants of Ruth and Boaz (4:17-22)

With very little trouble, I have prepared a simple outline of the Book of Ruth. The entire process (including three readings of the book itself) took me about an hour and a half. It gave me a personal acquaintance with the Book of Ruth and, as you can see, a handy summary on paper for my future reference.

The next chapter will discuss the type of Bible version that's best suited to deductive Bible study. Also use a Bible dictionary, encyclopedia, or handbook to find the meaning of unfamiliar biblical names. (For example, you would find that "Judah" in Ruth 1:7 does not refer to the *nation* Judah, which was created by the civil war in Rehoboam's day. That would occur centuries after the time of Ruth. So here the name "Judah" refers to the *territory* that was allotted to the tribe of Judah when the Israelites first entered the Promised Land.)

An exegetical or expository commentary will give you further insight into the cultural background of the Bible book you are studying. (For example, such a commentary's notes on Ruth 3 should tell you that Boaz was following the law of levitate marriage in marrying his kinsman's widow. The commentator then will explain what "levitate marriage" was.) You could also compare your personal assumptions about the authorship and time of writing with the conclusions in these commentaries. Compare your study notes about the writer's purpose and your outline of the book with those you find in a Bible survey or Bible introduction, respectively. Don't be surprised if you disagree with the experts now and then. But if you find a wide disparity, take a closer look at the Bible book itself; you may have missed something important.

For further instruction in using the deductive method of Bible study, see Joseph M. Gettys' "How to Study" series published by Westminster John Knox Press.[8] At the end of each chapter, Gettys provides an exercise in "Original Study," which uses the deductive method, and another exercise in "Advanced Study," which uses the inductive method of Bible study.

A Microscope: The Inductive (Analytical) Method

This method has become popular in recent years as lay readers have taken a keen interest in higher-critical Bible scholarship. The inductive method is a rather simple approach to high criticism. It is most useful for analyzing smaller sections of a Bible book (chapters, verses, even sentences), in order to detect subtle nuances in the writer's message or mood. So we could call this method the "microscope" approach.

Various authors have devoted entire books to the inductive method of Bible study.[9] Perhaps we should refer to these *methods* of Bible study, because the various authors recommend a wide variety of techniques. The method I will describe here is not as elaborate as some, but I think it will give you a good idea of how you can pursue inductive Bible study.

Howard F. Vos defines inductive Bible study as "the process of reasoning or drawing conclusions from particular cases."[10] Inductive study begins where the deductive method ends. While deductive study will give you a composite picture of a Bible book or chapter, inductive study analyzes the various parts that make up the picture. After surveying the "big picture" of the entire book or chapter, you should analyze its component parts to understand

---

[8]The series includes *How to Study Luke, How to Study Acts, How to Study 1 Corinthians, How to Study Ephesians,* and *How to Study Revelation.*

[9]The classic texts on this subject are Daniel P. Fuller, *The Inductive Method of Bible Study,* 3rd ed. (Pasadena: Fuller Theological Seminary, 1959); Irving L. Jensen, *Independent Bible Study* (Chicago: Moody, 1963); Grant R. Osborne and Stephen B. Woodward, *Handbook for Bible Study* (Ada, MI: Baker Book House, 1979), chaps. 7–9; and David L. Thompson, *Bible Study That Works* (Nappanee: Evangel, 1994).

[10]Vos, *Effective Bible Study,* 16.

how the writer conveys that theme and why the writer has used certain terms to communicate the message. Daniel J. Fuller observes that such an attempt "requires fatiguing and often discouraging effort,"[11] but the insights are well worth the effort.

Bible teachers disagree about how large a portion of Scripture you should consider as the basic unit for inductive study. Jensen and Vos believe the paragraph is the basic unit. Fuller says each proposition (statement) is the basic unit. Osborne and Woodward feel that each phrase or clause should be considered. Here we will use the paragraph, since it is the largest of these units, so our notes will be easier to manage when we begin diagraming our work. (If you try to diagram each phrase, or even each statement, you will generate several pages of notes for each chapter you are studying. That is too cumbersome.)

Let's analyze the Book of Ruth, paragraph by paragraph. You will need a Bible version that divides the text into topical paragraphs, not one that treats every verse as a paragraph. Notice the paragraph indentations that signal the start of new paragraphs. (Some Bible versions indent every verse, but signify the start of a topical paragraph by printing that verse number in bold type.)

Each version with paragraph formatting divides the biblical material in its own way. The NRSV has 15 paragraphs in the Book of Ruth. The New Living Translation has 48. The NIV has 55. Obviously, the editors of these various versions had their own ideas about how to organize this book!

Let's say you choose the NRSV for this study. It gives you 16 basic units of thought to analyze. The inductive study notes (Figure 3) show how you might set up your notebook pages for the work. Let me explain how to use them.

First, in the top two rows of each page, identify the *UNITS* you are considering. In this example, you are looking at paragraphs, so you write "¶" (symbol for paragraph) and its respective number in the sequence. Directly below that, you write the Scripture reference for that paragraph.[12] If you were studying verses, you could

---

[11]Fuller, *The Inductive Method of Bible Study*, IV-2.

[12]You can use this notebook format for any basic unit of study. Although we have used the NRSV's paragraph structure in this example, you can choose whatever unit that seems appropriate for your particular study. Inductive Bible study is a flexible method, even though it requires painstaking care.

write "Verse 1—Verse 2 —Verse 3" and so on in the top row, and would not need to fill in the second row. If you were considering propositions (statements), phrases, or clauses, you would give each of these units an identification number in the top row and show the verse where it appears in the second row. This same format can be used with any size unit.

Second, note in your own words the *CONTENT* of that unit. Two questions will help you do this: "What happens?" or, "Who speaks, and what does he/she say?" If you are studying a doctrinal book (such as one of Paul's epistles) in which there is no real action, you might answer two different questions: "What does he say?" and "Why must he say it?" In any case, make your notes concise and clear.

Third, note any *ODD PHRASE* that appears in the passage; I've allowed room for three of these. By an "odd phrase," I mean a word or phrase that (1) is unfamiliar to you, (2) seems ironic or contradictory in the context, or (3) seems to have a double meaning of some sort. After you have noted these, refer to the appropriate Bible reference book to find the meaning of each phrase. If it's simply an unfamiliar word (such as "Ephrathite" in ¶1), look it up in a Bible dictionary or encyclopedia. If you encounter an unusual English word—one that is not strictly biblical terminology (such as "gleaner" in ¶5)—you probably can find the meaning in any English dictionary. For an unfamiliar biblical phrase (such as, "May the Lord do thus and so to me, and more as well" in ¶3), you may need to check an expository or exegetical commentary on this passage—one that explains the meaning of every phrase in the text. Such a commentary may also help you understand a phrase that seems ironic or contradictory (such as "judges ruled" in ¶1). To check the meaning of unusual words, try a Bible dictionary or encyclopedia (for proper names like "Naomi") or an exegetical commentary (for common words used in unusual ways, such as the reference to God's "wings" in ¶6). Use a Bible handbook to get information about unusual customs (such as "dip your morsel in the sour wine, ¶7), foreign currency or measurements (such as the "ephah" in ¶8 or "measure" in ¶11), and other miscellaneous facts that you cannot find elsewhere (such as "maintaining the name" in ¶12 and wives' status as property in ¶13).

Fourth, summarize the *MAJOR IDEA* or *EVENT* in the paragraph. Look again at your notes under *CONTENT* and choose the central

Swords and Whetstones

Figure 3–Inductive Bible Study Notes

INDUCTIVE BIBLE STUDY NOTES

UNIT	91	92	93	94
TEXT	Ruth 1:1-5	Ruth 1:6-14	Ruth 1:15-18	Ruth 1:19-21
CONTENT What happens?	Elimelech's family goes to Moab, Elimelech dies; 2 sons marry + die.	Naomi plans return; urges Orpah & Ruth to stay in Moab; Orpah does.	Naomi again urges Ruth to stay; Ruth insists on going w/ her.	They return to Bethlehem; Naomi laments her plight.
Who speaks, and what does he/she say?	—	Naomi- I am too old to have a husband. (vv. 11-13)	Ruth - "Where you go I will go." (v. 16)	Women - Is this Naomi? Naomi- "Call me Mara." (v. 20)
ODD PHRASE Meaning	judges ruled (1:1) - led volunteer armies	Orpah (v.14) Heb., 'youthful'	May the Lord do thus (v 17) -oath to die.	Naomi (v 19) Heb., 'pleasant'
ODD PHRASE Meaning	Ephrathite (1:2) - native of Bethlehem	Ruth (v.14) Heb., 'friendly'	—	Mara (v. 20) Heb., 'bitter'
ODD PHRASE Meaning	—	—	—	—
MAJOR IDEA/EVENT	Naomi's husband + sons die.	Naomi urges girls to stay.	Ruth insists on going w/ Naomi.	Naomi laments her plight.
UNRESOLVED QUESTIONS	Why didn't family return to Judah?	Why should they seek shelter in mother's house and husband's house?	—	Why did Naomi blame God?
Answers	Because they had not heard famine was over (1:6).		—	Later blessed Him (2:20). Blessing proved (4:14-17).

Figure 3–Inductive Bible Study Notes (Continued)

INDUCTIVE BIBLE STUDY NOTES

UNIT	𝒜5	𝒜6	𝒜7	𝒜8
TEXT	Ruth 1:22-2:7	Ruth 2:8-13	Ruth 2:14-16	Ruth 2:17-23
CONTENT What happens?	Ruth gleans barley; enters field of Boaz, husband's kin; he sees her.	Boaz invites Ruth to stay in his field.	Boaz invites Ruth to meal, tells workers to leave grain for her.	Ruth brings grain to Naomi; tells her of Boaz.
Who speaks, and what does he/she say?	Boaz - "To whom does this young woman belong?" (v5).	Boaz - "I have ordered the young men not to bother you" (v. 9).	Boaz - "Dip your morsel in the sour wine" (v. 14).	Naomi - "The Lord has not forsaken the living or the dead" (v.20).
ODD PHRASE Meaning	gleaner - one who salvages grain	she fell on her face - custom of respect	dip your morsel - custom of hospitality	ephah - about 1.1 bushel
ODD PHRASE Meaning	Boaz (2:1) - Heb., 'swiftness'	God's "wings" - His protection	—	"you might be bothered" - raped
ODD PHRASE Meaning	—	—	—	—
MAJOR IDEA/EVENT	Boaz notices Ruth.	Boaz invites Ruth to stay.	Boaz tells workers to leave grain.	Ruth tells of Boaz.
UNRESOLVED QUESTIONS	—	Did harvesters often molest the gleaners?	Why note that she had food left over?	How long did barley & wheat harvests last?
Answers	—	Apparently (2:22)	She would take it to Naomi (v. 18)	

Copyright © 1982, 1999 Joseph D. Allison

           Swords and Whetstones

Figure 3–Inductive Bible Study Notes (Continued)

INDUCTIVE BIBLE STUDY NOTES

UNIT	#9	#10	#11	#12
TEXT	Ruth 3:1-5	Ruth 3:6-13	Ruth 3:14-18	Ruth 4:1-6
CONTENT What happens?	Naomi tells Ruth to seek home w/ Boaz.	Ruth lays herself beside Boaz, offers to be his wife; he tells of nearer kin.	Ruth returns to Naomi w/ news; Naomi tells her to wait.	Boaz offers next kin chance to buy land + marry Ruth; he declines.
Who speaks, and what does he/she say?	Naomi - "Go and uncover his feet and lie down."	Boaz - "You have not gone after younger men" (v.10).	Naomi - He "will settle the matter today." (see #5)	Boaz - "The day you acquire the field, you are also acquiring Ruth" (v.5).
ODD PHRASE Meaning	—	"act as next-of-kin" (v.13) - duty to marry relative's widow	six measures- 6 x 6.9 quarts	"maintain the name..." (v5) w/o children the family name dies.
ODD PHRASE Meaning	—	—	—	—
ODD PHRASE Meaning	—	—	—	—
MAJOR IDEA/EVENT	Naomi tells Ruth to seek home w/ Boaz.	Ruth offers to be Boaz's wife.	Ruth tells Naomi the news.	Next of kin declines offer.
UNRESOLVED QUESTIONS	Why should she lie down w/ him?	What was Ruth's "first" kindness (v.10)?	Why keep Ruth's visit a secret (v.14)?	—
Answers	Custom of betrothal - he had to spread his skirt over her (v.9).	What she did for Naomi (2:11).		

Figure 3–Inductive Bible Study Notes (Continued)

INDUCTIVE BIBLE STUDY NOTES				
UNIT	9 13	9 14	9 15	
TEXT	Ruth 4:7-12	Ruth 4:13-17	Ruth 4:18-22	
CONTENT What happens?	Boaz buys the land + takes Ruth as his wife.	Ruth bears a son; women congratulate Naomi; she nurses him as her own.	A list of the descendants of Boaz and Ruth.	
Who speaks, and what does he/she say?	—	Women - Ruth "is more to you than 7 sons" (v.15).		
ODD PHRASE Meaning	"I have also acquired Ruth" (v.10) - wives considered property	Obed (v.17) - Heb., 'servant.'	descendants of Perez (v.18) Chief tribal ancestor.	
ODD PHRASE Meaning	Name ... not cut off from the gate (v.10) - family reps. sat at city gate.	—	—	
ODD PHRASE Meaning	like Perez (v.12) - eldest son of Judah (i.e., chief heir).	—	—	
MAJOR IDEA/EVENT	Boaz takes Ruth as his wife.	Ruth bears a son.	List of descendants	
UNRESOLVED QUESTIONS	—	Is verse 16 literal? Can an old woman give suck?		
Answers				

event or idea there. This strip of the chart makes a more detailed—and more accurate—outline of the book than you could achieve with the deductive study method.

Finally, note any *UNRESOLVED QUESTIONS* posed by this passage: Does the writer say something that puzzles you? (See ¶9 and ¶14.) Does he refer to some other person or incident in Scripture, without fully explaining what he means? (See ¶1 and ¶10.) Does he raise some other question without answering it here? (See ¶4, ¶6, ¶9.) Note these questions at this point and look for an answer *in the Scriptures*. Scripture is its own best interpreter.

Even after reading the entire book, some questions may not be resolved, and you may need to consult a commentary or other reference book for someone else's interpretation. The type of question will determine the book you use. Generally, for interpreting an unusual word or phrase (see ¶2) you should consult an exegetical or expository commentary (assuming the expository treatment is detailed enough). For interpreting matters of doctrine, history, or motive (see ¶11), an expository or devotional commentary should help. And for questions of culture, social customs, and the like (see ¶8), consult a Bible encyclopedia or Bible handbook.

Your notes are important to the inductive method because the note-taking process: (1) forces you to fix a critical eye on every phrase of the text, (2) allows you to gather bits of information that you find along the way, and (3) gives you a permanent record of what you learn, for future review. I suggest that you make the inductive notes in ink, since you probably will not need to reorganize them in light of subsequent reading and you will have a more legible, durable record.

Doing the Word

Irving L. Jensen points out that no method of Bible study is complete without *interpretation* and *application* of what we find.[13] I heartily agree. We need to grasp the meaning of what the Bible says (interpretation) and begin changing our lives to conform to what it says (application) if Scripture is to have any real value for our daily lives.

---

[13]Jensen, *Independent Bible Study*, pp. 157-58.

For if anyone is a hearer of the word and not a doer, he is like a man observing his natural face in a mirror; for he observes himself, goes away, and immediate forgets what kind of man he was. But he who looks into the perfect law of liberty and continues in it, and is not a forgetful hearer but a doer of the word, this one will be blessed in what he does (James 1:23-25).

In this chapter I have presented some simple, practical methods for studying the Word of God. If you faithfully use these methods, you should be able to comprehend what the Word says. But then you have responsibility to live according to the Word. No Bible study method or library of resources can show you how to do that, but the Holy Spirit can. And I believe He will!

ANNOTATED BIBLIOGRAPHY

Arnold, Jeffrey. *Discovering the Bible for Yourself.* Downers Grove, IL: InterVarsity Press, 1993.

The saying is now familiar: "Give a man a fish and you feed him for a day. Teach a man to fish and you feed him for a lifetime." Jeffrey Arnold's objective in this book is to give Christian laymen the skills to study God's Word for themselves. He teaches us how to "fish" for the spiritual nourishment in Scripture by using inductive Bible Study. Arnold's narrative is friendly and inviting. He encourages the reader to try the techniques of inductive study in a small group, where there's opportunity to gain perspective from other eager students of the Word. This simple handbook provides a practical way to begin "discovering the Bible for yourself."

Cunningham, Phillip J. *Exploring Scripture: How the Bible Came to Be.* New York: Paulist Press, 1992.

A Roman Catholic layperson's introduction to textual criticism, *Exploring Scripture* grew out of Professor Cunningham's years of university teaching experience. He hopes to give the reader some analytical tools to separate myth from historical facts in the Bible. He manages to avoid mind-numbing digressions into complex theories of how the Bible was compiled. Most Christians will find this to be a valuable overview of the field, though fundamentalists will be offended by Cunningham's simplistic dismissal of their views.

Fee, Gordon D. and Douglas Stuart. *How to Read the Bible for All It's Worth: A Guide to Understanding the Bible*, second ed. Grand Rapids: Zondervan, 1993.

When you are ready to learn about various types of Bible literature and how those genres should inform the interpretation of each passage, this book will orient you to that world. Professors Fee and Stuart manage to explain the inner techniques of Scripture interpretation in a way that any intelligent layperson will understand. They introduce technical terms sparingly and systematically. The result is a textbook that beginning college students will appreciate as much as lay readers do.

Hsu, Jeffrey. *Computer Bible Study*. Dallas: Word, 1993.

If you have never used a personal computer to facilitate your Bible study, Hsu's book introduces you to the basics of this growing field. He clearly describes the various kinds of Bible reference software that you can use. The "how-to" chapters of this book introduce the novice computer user to this fascinating study tool. The greatest deficiency of the book is its concluding "Bible Software Reference" section, which reviews several dozen software programs. This section now is sadly outdated.

Littleton, Mark R. *Delighted by Discipline*. Wheaton, IL: Chariot Victor Books, 1990.

We don't use Scripture memorization as a Bible study tool as often as Christians did a generation ago. But Littleton shares how Scripture memorization can enrich a Christian's life, even in this microchip age. He emphasizes not only how to memorize the Word, but how to apply the Word when the Lord recalls it to mind. This simple, anecdotal book brings encouragement to any Christian who wants to learn more of the Bible.

Peace, Richard. *Contemplative Bible Reading: Experiencing God Through Scripture*. Colorado Springs: NavPress, 1998.

Dr. Peace of Fuller Theological Seminary has written this practical guide to *lectio divina**, the practice of contemplative Bible study. Roman Catholics (especially those who follow the spiritual disciplines of St. Benedict) have practiced this type of devotional study for centuries. Only in recent years have Protestants begun to appreciate it. Dr. Peace explains how to do contemplative

Bible study individually or in a small group. The book is organized for ten sessions of study, with a group leader's guide at the end.

Richards, Lawrence O. *99 Ways to Start a Study Group and Keep It Growing.* Grand Rapids: Zondervan, 1987.

One of the most practical books on small-group ministry, Richards' manual places Scripture at the center of the group's study and discussion. He provides dozens of activities that a small group can use to explore and apply the Word to daily life. Just as important, he describes the five elements of a healthy small-group ministry, so that the leader can read the group's vital signs, week after week.

Chapter 2

Bible Versions

We English-speaking people have two ways to read the Bible. We can learn the original languages in which it was written (biblical Hebrew, *koine Greek**, and a smattering of Aramaic), or we can use an English *translation** of the Bible. A German housewife who would like to read *Gone with the Wind* has similar choices. She can learn the English language or get a translation in German. But there the similarity would end, for translating the Bible into English is quite different from translating a twentieth-century novel into a foreign language. When you understand the difference, you will understand why we have so many English versions of the Bible.

Someone translating *Gone with the Wind* into German can still refer to first-edition English copies of the novel. However, someone who wants to translate the Bible has no first-edition copies. The best we have available are handwritten copies made at least 150 years after the original manuscript was written. And the Bible translator finds perplexing differences among these various copies. For example, some copies of John 1:34 say that Jesus is "the Son of God" (per the KJV and NIV), while others say He is "God's Chosen One" (NEB). Which one should a translator follow in making the English rendition?

Someone must evaluate these Bible manuscript copies in order to choose the ones that seem most authentic. We refer to this task of picking and choosing as *textual criticism** or *lower criticism** and it is quite a sophisticated science.

Anyone who wants to translate *Gone with the Wind* into German is working with two current, known languages, but someone who translates the Bible must deal with several ancient languages as well as a modern language. The Bible translator must interpret languages that have not been spoken for centuries, whose vocabulary and rules of grammar have been lost. Occasionally, the translator must compare biblical words with words in other ancient languages to try to guess their meaning. Then he must try to convey that meaning into modern English.

29

A person translating *Gone with the Wind* into German is handling a literary work, written primarily to entertain us. Someone who wants to translate the Bible is handling a spiritual work, which God gave us to explain the way to live. If the translator of the novel fails to grasp all of author Margaret Mitchell's meaning, the readers of the novel will still have an enjoyable experience. If the translator of the Bible fails to grasp all of God's meaning, the consequences would be more serious. So the Bible translator must be very careful to convey the sense of the original and to avoid including any personal theological views.

English Versions: A Capsule History

English translations (*versions**) of the Bible have been made for almost thirteen hundred years. The work began with Bishop Aldhelm of Sherborne, who translated the Psalms into Old English shortly before his death in the year 709. The Venerable Bede, a learned Christian monk at Jarrow, translated part of the Gospel of John into Old English before he died in 735. By the tenth century, Old English scholars had translated all of the Gospels and large portions of the Old Testament into their language.[1]

The man who first brought the entire Bible into English was John Wycliffe of Oxford. Wycliffe felt that the common people needed to understand God's Word, and he knew that reading the Scriptures in their own language would greatly aid their understanding. So from his post as a lecturer at Oxford University, Wycliffe encouraged scholars of the Oxford community to begin the work of translating the Bible into English.

The printing press had not yet been invented, so these men had to "publish" their work as handwritten manuscripts. They completed the translation shortly before Wycliffe's death in 1384. (Note that Wycliffe's team did not work from the oldest Hebrew and Greek manuscript copies; they used a Latin translation called the Vulgate, made by the Roman Catholic scholar Jerome around A.D. 400. The manuscripts that Jerome had used were themselves late copies of the original manuscripts. So Wycliffe's version was a translation of a translation...of a copy!)

---

[1]F. F. Bruce gives a more detailed account of this early translating process in his *History of the Bible in English*, 3rd ed. (New York: Oxford University Press, 1978), 1–11.

More than sixty years later (ca. 1450), Johann Gutenberg invented the process of printing with moveable type. Up to this time, printers carved the printing plate for an entire page of printed matter from a single block of wood, which was a slow, tedious process. But Gutenberg learned how to cast metal molds of individual letters of the alphabet, then locked these letters together to make a complete page. After finishing a job, he could rearrange the metal letters to make a new page. This was the breakthrough that made modern printing possible.

Gutenberg's new technology deluged the Christian world with various editions of the Greek and Hebrew texts, along with new editions of the Latin version and new versions in other languages. Martin Luther released his German New Testament in 1522 and the complete German Bible in 1534. William Tyndale published his English New Testament in 1526. Miles Coverdale published an entire English Bible in 1535.

The sixteenth century brought many other English versions, including the Matthew's Bible (1537), the Great Bible (1539), the Geneva Bible (1560), and the Bishops' Bible (1568). In addition to these Protestant efforts, Roman Catholic translators produced the Rheims New Testament (1582) and the Douay Old Testament in 1609-10 in French.

Then came the King James Version of 1611. We call it the King James Version (KJV) or "Authorized Version" because King James I of England authorized the project. His six teams of translators worked from printed *critical editions** of the New Testament (which had been made using manuscripts no older than the Middle Ages) and from earlier English versions such as Tyndale's translation. For the Old Testament, they used a Hebrew critical edition, while consulting a third-century B.C. Greek version known as the *Septuagint** and the earlier English versions. In the preface to their work, the KJV translators said: "We never thought from the beginning that we should need to make a new translation, nor yet to make of a bad one a good one—but to make a good one better...."[2]

The "good" translation that they hoped to improve was the Bishops' Bible of 1568, which was preferred by the Anglican cler-

---

[2]Joseph L. Gardner. ed., *Reader's Digest Atlas of the Bible* (Pleasantville, NY: Reader's Digest Association. 1981), 29.

gy. The most popular Bible of the masses was the Geneva Bible of 1560, produced by English scholars who had escaped to Geneva during the persecutions of Queen Mary. It was printed in a handy size and with clear Roman type. King James I hoped that the new version would satisfy not only the Anglican clergy, but the Puritan reformers and the uneducated public as well.

The King James Version enjoyed several advantages over the earlier English versions of the Bible:

(1) It was sanctioned by the King of England, thus assuring that most English-speaking people could use it. Many previous English versions had been suppressed by government officials.

(2) It was published after printers had perfected Gutenberg's process, which permitted them to make fairly inexpensive copies of the KJV.

(3) Its translators held various theological views, giving the project a system of "checks and balances" to override sectarian theological biases.

(4) Its translators were masters of the English language, so they could phrase their work in prose of exquisite beauty.

Yet not all of the people of England liked the new translation. The Pilgrims would not even allow a copy of the KJV on board the Mayflower when it sailed for the New World nine years later; because they accepted only the Geneva Bible.[3]

Despite this grudging welcome, the KJV came to be accepted as the standard English Bible version of its day—indeed, the standard version of the following centuries.[4]

Lower Criticism

In later centuries, scholars discovered many Bible manuscripts that were older than the ones used by the KJV translators. The scholars have used these older manuscripts to compile *critical editions** of the Hebrew and Greek Testaments.

---

[3]Eugene H. Glassman, *The Translation Debate* (Downers Grove, IL: InterVarsity, 1981), 15.

[4]However, the King James Version as we have it today is not the King James Version of 1611, even though the title page of your KJV may say that it is. Publishers have revised the text of the KJV several times, and the Bible now known as the King James Version is a revision made in 1762 by Dr. Thomas Parris of Cambridge and in 1769 by Dr. Benjamin Blayney of Oxford.

This brings us into the arena of *biblical criticism** —the task of evaluating Bible manuscripts and the content of Scripture itself, using a variety of methods. A long discussion of critical methods is not necessary at this point. But to understand the differences between modern Bible versions, we need to understand the process of textual criticism, which is also called *lower criticism.**[5]

Imagine that the discipline of biblical criticism is a hotel building with several stories. If delivery couriers wish to take a package to someone who lives on an upper story, they must enter at the ground level and be admitted by a security guard. In the "hotel" of biblical criticism, the lower level with its cautious guard is textual criticism. The upper levels, where the package is used by scholars employing the various methods of studying the Bible, are called *higher criticism.**

Lower criticism is fundamental to all types of Bible study. Before we consider the meaning of Scripture, we must be sure that we are using a text that best preserves what the original writer set down. We must be sure that it is genuine Scripture. Or, to use the hotel analogy, we must let our "security guard" (the textual critic) check the contents of the package (manuscript).

In the nineteenth and early twentieth centuries, archaeologists began finding older Bible manuscripts in the Middle East. Researchers found other long-forgotten manuscripts in neglected corners of their European archives. As textual critics compared manuscripts, they found that each one had flaws. Words or entire phrases were missing, marred, or obviously rewritten. So the textual critics compiled what seemed to be the most authentic material from these manuscripts in order to provide more reliable Bible texts. Each reconstructed text is called a critical edition or *critical text.*[6] The textual critics (the "security guards" of the Scripture text) compiled several new critical editions in the two centuries following the translation of the KJV.

---

[5]For a brief description of higher criticism, see Chapter 6.

[6]Textual scholars ("critics") produce the "critical text" by comparing several Bible manuscripts. Translators then work from the critical text to produce the version we use in our language. Anyone reading an English version should ask, "What critical text(s) did the translator use?"

The Call for a Revised Version

Serious Bible students began calling for a thorough revision of the KJV, using these critical editions in the late 1800's. Lay readers also wanted someone to revise the KJV for a different reason— they wanted a Bible version in a modern English idiom they could understand.

The Church of England appointed a group of scholars to make such a revision. The group issued their version of the New Testament in 1881 and the Old Testament in 1885. Together, these became known as the English Revised Version or simply the Revised Version (RV). The Church of England permitted a group of American scholars to issue their own edition of this work, because the Americans hoped to modify the translation a bit to better reflect American usage.

While the translators were doing this, a young German made a stunning discovery. Adolf Deissmann, an instructor at the University of Marburg, was reviewing some Greek papyrus letters at Heidelberg University one day in 1895 when he realized that the common (*koine*) Greek language used in these secular letters resembled New Testament Greek.

Until this time, Bible scholars thought that the New Testament used a *dialect** all its own. In fact, some referred to it as "biblical Greek." They could not discern the meaning of some New Testament words, because they could not find where these words were used elsewhere. They had pored over the sophisticated writings of classical Greek literature without finding them. But Adolf Deissmann found plenty of other occurrences of these "New Testament Greek" words in the everyday letters of that ancient time.

Unfortunately, Deissmann's discovery came too late to help the American translators, who published their edition of the RV in 1901. They called this new version the American Standard Version (ASV).

But Deissmann's discovery and further manuscript finds prompted publication of other English versions after the ASV. In fact, John H. Skilton lists 123 new versions of the New Testament or the entire Bible issued between 1881 and 1973,[7] and many oth-

---

[7]John H. Skilton, ed., *The New Testament Student at Work*, vol. 2 (Phillipsburg, NJ: Presbyterian and Reformed, 1975), 217-20.

ers have appeared in the quarter-century since then. Almost every new version has attempted to improve upon the accuracy or style of the versions that have come before. At the end of this chapter, you will find a list of some better English versions now available. Figure 4 compares some of these versions.

Many Versions—A Curse or a Blessing?

Any Christian pastor has heard the complaint: "Why must we have so many versions of the Bible? Why can't we agree on one translation and stop turning out so many 'new and improved' models?" It's a legitimate question. Certainly, there are some disadvantages to having so many versions of the Bible.

Consider what happens in a typical worship service. The pastor reads the text for the morning sermon, and the furrowed brows of people in the congregation indicates they are reading several different versions. He might say, "Now the New Revised Standard Version renders it this way," or, "The New American Standard Bible throws a different light on that verse by rendering it this way." Even with these explanations, some parishioners will comment after the service, "I didn't understand your point about verse 12. My Bible doesn't say that!"

Of course, a preacher cannot compare a variety of Bible versions in every sermon. Normally, one must take a single version for the day's text and plunge ahead with the sermon, disregarding those furrowed brows and complaints. (Yet I don't think we would like to return to the days of the Bishops' Bible, when each church had only one large Bible chained beneath the pulpit, so that laypeople could take turns consulting it while the pastor preached!)

Another disadvantage of having so many versions is the incompatibility of Bible study aids. For example, you cannot buy a concordance that will work with all versions of the Bible. A concordance is based on the KJV, the NRSV, the NIV, or some other version. If you remember part of a verse from the KJV and try to find the verse in an NIV concordance, the NIV's wording may be different enough to sidetrack you. You will encounter similar problems in the use of commentaries based on a version different from that of your Bible. Or try using a modern Bible dictionary as

Figure 4–Comparison of Versions

Version	Date	Text Used	Number of Translators
American Standard Version	1901	O.T.–Jacob ben Chayim's text (1524-25)[1] N.T.–Westcott & Hort's critical edition (1881)	30
Amplified Bible	O.T. 1965 N.T. 1958	O.T.–Rudolf Kittel's *Biblia Hebraica*[2] N.T.–Westcott & Hort's critical edition (1881)	12
King James Version	1611	O.T.–Jacob ben Chayim's text (1524-25)[1] consulting the LXX N.T.–Theodore Beza's *Textus Receptus*	47
Living Bible	1970	ASV (Paraphrase)	1
New American Standard Bible	1971	O.T.–Rudolf Kittel's *Biblia Hebraica*[2] N.T.–Nestle's critical (23rd ed.)	58
New International Version	O.T. 1978 N.T. 1973	O.T.–Rudolf Kittel's *Biblia Hebraica*[2] N.T.–Eclectic text	108
New Jerusalem Bible	1988	Translation of *La Bible de Jerusalem*, with the aid of the Latin Vulgate and various Greek and Hebrew texts	28
New King James Version	O.T. 1982 N.T. 1979	O.T.–Jacob ben Chayim's text,[1] consulting the LXX N.T.–F.H.A. Scrivener's *Textus Receptus*	119
New Living Translation	1996	O.T.–*Biblia Hebraica Stuttgartensia* (1977) N.T.–Aland/Black/Metzger critical (4th) ed. and Nestle's critical (27th) ed.	92
New Revised Standard Version	1989	O.T.–*Biblia Hebraica Stuttgartensia* (1977) N.T.–Aland/Black/Metzger critical (3rd) ed.	30
Revised English Bible	1989	O.T.–Rudolf Kittel's *Biblia Hebraica*[2] N.T.–Eclectic text	50
Revised Standard Version	O.T. 1952 N.T. 1946	O.T.–Rudolf Kittel's *Biblia Hebraica*[2] N.T.–Westcott & Hort's critical ed. (1881)	32
Today's English Version	O.T. 1974 N.T. 1966	O.T.–Rudolf Kittel's *Biblia Hebraica*[2] N.T.–Aland/Black/Metzger's critical ed.	1

[1]Revised in the Antwerp Polyglot (1569-72).
[2]Third edition (1937), based on the Leningrad Manuscript (A.D. 1008) of the Masoretic Text, edited by Aaron ben Moshe ben Asher.

you study the KJV and look up words like *sackbut* or *adamant.* You won't find them!

We might list other disadvantages to having many versions of the Bible, but the problems are not insurmountable. For example, a congregation can address the problem of using different versions in a worship service by having pew Bibles of the same version. Worshipers will still refer to their own versions, of course; but they can follow the pew Bible as the pastor reads the sermon text. An individual can overcome the problem of incompatible study aids by choosing one version for serious study and then buying the study aids designed for that version. Other solutions are available.

For a moment, consider the other side of the issue. Are there any advantages to having many English versions of the Bible? Indeed there are.

First, the various Bible versions help to balance one another theologically. I mentioned earlier that a translator should avoid bringing personal theological views into the work; but if you compare different versions very carefully, you will find a definite theological perspective in each one. Figure 5 shows how several translators have rendered a few texts. Notice the theological stance of each one. Also notice how limited your understanding of each verse would be if you had only one version to consult.

Second, the various versions can offset weaknesses in the methods of translation. The two basic methods of translation are *formal equivalence** and *dynamic equivalence.** A translator who tries to achieve formal equivalence will pick words and phrases that closely match the meaning of original manuscripts. The goal is to give us an English-language "mirror image" of the Hebrew and Greek originals—the same thought pattern, perhaps even the same level of sophistication and the same cadence (rhythm of reading) that you would find in the original text. However, English is quite unlike Hebrew or Greek. So when a translator tries to give us formal equivalence, the English style must be forced into a Hebrew or Greek mold. The result may be hard to understand.

On the other hand, a translator who tries to achieve dynamic equivalence will try to express the meaning in modern English style, even if it means restructuring the original thought pattern of the passage. The weakness of this method is that the translator may give us a distorted or partial view of what the passage really says. Another problem with this method is that the dynamic-equivalence translator tries to express these ideas in a current, modern idiom. Thus, the version will be out of date in a few years, as the idioms and clichés pass from use.[8]

To get the full impact of a Bible passage, read a formal-equivalence version beside a dynamic-equivalence version. One may clarify the meaning of the other. One may also rein in distortions or exaggerations of the other.

On the other hand, be careful when comparing two dynamic-equivalence versions. They may give two radically different views of a passage! (See the comparison in Figure 6.)

Another advantage of having many versions is that they help to convey the meaning of the Bible to various communities of the English-speaking world. The English language as it is spoken in the hills of eastern Tennessee has its own jargon and shades of meanings, quite different from what we find on the streets of London. This is why the English Revised Version of 1881 was not suitable for the United States. It's also why a separate British edition of *The Living Bible* was published when that paraphrase first appeared. Each translation has its intended audience and the translators phrase their work in the dialect of their audience.

We should thank God for our generous supply of English Bible versions. With them, we can discover the subtle nuances of the ancient Bible manuscripts, even if we cannot read Greek and Hebrew for ourselves. We can plumb the depths of Bible theology, even if we cannot articulate an intricate theology of our own. We can read and understand the Word of God in the same terms we use in everyday conversation. Only when we understand the Word can the Word change our lives.

---

[8]Some people call any dynamic-equivalence version a "paraphrase," as Eugene H. Glassman does in his book, *The Translation Debate*. But that is misleading. Strictly speaking, a paraphrase takes a translated version and restates it in other, simpler words in the same language. In this respect, *The Living Bible* was a true paraphrase, because the translator (Kenneth Taylor) took one English version and rephrased it in English terms. His editors did check his work against the Greek and Hebrew manuscripts; but for the most part, *The Living Bible* was the ASV in modern clothing—a paraphrase.

Selecting Versions to Study

As your own spiritual needs change from time to time, your method of Bible study should change as well. Be alert to find the Bible version(s) best suited to the type of study you are doing now. We explored three Bible study methods in the previous chapter. Let's think now about how to select the Bible version that's appropriate to each of these methods.

1. *Devotional Bible Study.* For the devotional method, select a Bible version that is clear and easy to understand. A dynamic-

Figure 5–Differing Theological Views

Text	Protestant Version	Roman Catholic Version
Matthew 19:9	...If a man divorces his wife for any cause other than unchastity, and marries another he commits adultery. (NEB)	...Whoever divorces his wife (lewd conduct is a separate case) and marries another commits adultery. (NAB)

Protestant translators usually believe this verse has an "exception clause"—i.e., they feel that Jesus condemns remarriage after divorce except when the divorce was caused by infidelity. Roman Catholic translators disagree. The NAB translators believe that "lewd conduct" is but simply one reason why some people seek divorce, but that does not excuse remarriage after divorce.

Text	Non-Charismatic View	Charismatic View
1 Corinthians 14:14-19	For if I pray in a tongue, my spirit prays but my mind is unproductive. What should I do then? I will pray with the spirit, but I will pray with the mind also; I will sing praise with the spirit, but I will sing praise with the mind also. (NRSV)	For if I pray in tongues, my spirit is praying, but I don't understand what I am saying. Well then, what shall I do? I will do both. I will pray in the spirit, and I will pray in words I understand. I will sing in the spirit, and I will sing in words I understand. (NLT)

The translators of the New Revised Standard Version follow the Greek text literally, even though it is ambiguous about the "tongues" that Paul describes. The translators of the New Living Translation assume Paul is referring to ecstatic prayer languages, which are unknown to any human being (including the person who speaks). They translate the text in a way that supports this belief.

equivalence version or paraphrase will be easier to read than a formal-equivalence version. Avoid a version that inserts several alternate readings into the text, such as the *Amplified Bible*, since this makes the train of thought very difficult to follow.

Try to find a paraphrase that accurately reflects the original meaning of the Hebrew and Greek texts. If you can't read Hebrew or Greek, here are a couple of clues to help you:

Figure 6–Differing Textual Bases and Translation Methods

Text	*Textus Receptus*	*Westcott-Hort Critical Ed.*
Luke 17:36	Two men will be in the field: the one will be taken and the other left (NKJV).	Omitted (NIV)

In this case, the Westcott-Hort critical edition completely omits a verse that is found in the Textus Receptus. The verse does not appear in the earliest Greek manuscripts, but it does appear in most Greek manuscripts copies made in the Middle Ages.

Text	*Textus Receptus*	*Westcott-Hort Critical Ed.*
1 John 5:7	For there are three that bear witness in heaven: the Father, the Word, and the Holy Spirit; and these three are one (NKJV).	There are three that testify: the Spirit and the water and the blood, and these three agree (NRSV).

Here the Westcott-Hort critical edition gives a completely different rendering of a verse than we find in the Textus Receptus. The "Father/Word/Spirit" rendering does not appear in the earliest Greek manuscripts, but it does appear in most copies that survive from the Middle Ages.

Text	*Formal Equivalence*	*Dynamic Equivalence*
Acts 3:16	And His name, through faith in his name, has made this man strong, whom you see and know. Yes, the faith which comes through Him has given him this perfect soundness in the presence of you all (NKVJ).	The name of Jesus has healed this man—-and you know how lame he was before. Faith in Jesus' name has caused this healing before your very eyes (NLT).

The Greek word order of this verse seems awkward to English-language readers. The formal-equivalence version follows the Greek, but the dynamic-equivalence version rephrases it to give a smoother rendition. The two versions convey the same idea, although the dynamic-equivalence version is easier to read.

(a) *Avoid a version that uses generous amounts of modern slang.* A slang expression may convey a vivid idea to you, but it's not likely to convey the full idea that the Bible writers had in mind.

(b) *Read cautiously any version that inserts the translator's explanation of a verse into the text itself.* This amounts to a commentary on the Bible, but appears to be Scripture itself. The *Good News Bible* and the *New Living Translation* have some unfortunate examples of this.

2. *Inductive Bible Study.* For the inductive method, it's even more important to choose a Bible version that is both clear and accurate. If possible, use one that breaks poetry sections into stanzas and prose sections into paragraphs.

Stanzas will show you the parallel lines of Hebrew poetry, so that you can study the word meanings revealed by Hebrew *parallelism.** Paragraphs will help you find complete theme thoughts, especially in complex theological books, such as the Epistle to the Romans. The King James Version does not provide stanza and paragraph format, only verses.[9] The *New Living Translation* breaks up prose into paragraphs, but it does not give stanzas of poetry. (Its loose translation of the Hebrew obscures the parallelism.) Other modern versions such as the New King James Version (NKJV), the NRSV, the Revised English Bible (REB), the NASB, and the NIV provide both stanzas and paragraphs.

3. *Deductive or Synthetic Bible Study.* Stanza and paragraph divisions are not crucial features for deductive Bible study. Here it's more important to select a version that preserves the unity of the book you are studying. Some modern versions, such as the NRSV, set aside sections of Scripture that the translators did not find in the oldest manuscripts (e.g., see Acts 8:37, Acts 24:7, and 1 Pet. 5:2). Others rearrange entire chapters to follow current theories of how the Scriptures were written (see the Book of Revelation in *The Anchor Bible* commentary series). This can be confusing in a deductive study.

---

[9]The Geneva Bible of 1560 was the first complete English Bible to break up the Scriptures into chapters and verses to help readers find a passage more easily. But these divisions are arbitrary; they often divide the Scripture in mid-sentence or mid-thought. We continue to use them because they now have four hundred years of tradition behind them.

At various times, you may employ all of these three basic methods of Bible study—devotional, inductive, and deductive—to help you achieve your particular Bible study goals. Be sure to select a Bible version that's well-suited to the particular study method you're using. In fact, your study will be enriched if you use more than one version.

A Word about the Apocrypha

Most Protestant readers are not familiar with the term *Apocrypha*.* The Apocrypha (sometimes called the Deuterocanonicals) is a set of ancient books or essays written between the time of the Old Testament and the New. All but one of these books (Second Esdras) appeared in the *Septuagint,** the standard Greek version of the Old Testament that Jerome compiled in the third century B.C. He translated the (Greek) Apocrypha into Latin and included it in his Vulgate version of the Bible, even though he questioned the spiritual authority of these books in his introduction to the Vulgate. In fact, Jerome distributed these books throughout the Old Testament, as the Septuagint translators had done.

Coverdale's English Bible (1535) brought the apocryphal books together and placed them between the Old and New Testaments. The King James Version (1611) followed this pattern.

However, the Puritans and other radical Protestant groups removed the Apocrypha from their English versions for three reasons: (1) They had been written at such a late date, compared to other books of the Bible. (2) They were not considered part of the Old Testament by Jewish scholars themselves (at the Council of Jamnia, ca. A.D. 90. (3) These books often contradicted the teachings of the rest of Scripture.[10] So even though the first edition of the King James Version included the Apocrypha, later editions of the KJV omitted them.

The Roman Catholic Church, the Church of England, and several mainline denominations of Protestant Christians still read and use the Apocrypha. The REB, certain editions of the NRSV, and all Roman Catholic versions contain the Apocrypha. Commentaries on the Apocrypha are also available.

---

[10]See Coverdale's comments about the Apocrypha, quoted by Bruce, HBE, 60-61. (See Bible Reference Bibliographies, p. xiv of this book.)

ANNOTATED BIBLIOGRAPHY

Here is a list of some of the best current English versions of the Bible. (I have also included a few versions of the New Testament alone.) They are listed alphabetically by the title of the version, since the titles are more commonly known than the translators. When several different publishers produce a certain version, I have noted only the publisher of the first edition. I have omitted older and less popular versions such as the ASV and Moffatt's translation.

Amplified Bible. Grand Rapids: Zondervan, 1965.

While most modern versions put alternate readings in footnotes or italics at the end of each verse, the *Amplified* inserts alternates into the text itself. The Lockman Foundation compiled this version to give Bible students a quick way of tracing the various possible readings of each verse. This version uses brackets, parentheses, and italics to insert the various readings. This tends to clutter the text, making the *Amplified Bible* confusing for most laypeople to use.

Contemporary English Version. Nashville: Thomas Nelson, 1995.

The American Bible Society produced this new translation to give readers a clear rendering of the Scriptures in everyday English prose, while maintaining the reverence of the KJV. *Inclusive language** is used instead of masculine pronouns wherever the sense of the text allows. For example, the KJV quotes Jesus as saying, "If any man will come after me, let him deny himself, and take up his cross, and follow me" (Matt. 16:24). The CEV restates it: "If any of you want to be my followers, you must forget about yourself. You must take up your cross and follow me." For its clarity and fidelity to the original text, the CEV is the best standard Bible translation of today.

Good News Bible. New York: American Bible Society, 1976.

Robert G. Bratcher prepared a translation of the New Testament into simple English for people who were learning English as a second language. The American Bible Society published this translation in 1966 with the title, *Good News for Modern Man*. The Bible Society then pressed on to make a translation of the full Bible.

Again, their primary goal was to make a simple version for people who know English only as a second language. The *Good News Bible* does not follow the Hebrew and Greek manuscripts phrase-for-phrase, but it conveys the basic sense of the Scriptures. This translation is also called Today's English Version (TEV).[11]

New Jerusalem Bible. Garden City, NY: Doubleday, 1985.

Beginning in 1948, l'Ecole Biblique et Archeologique in Jerusalem published a massive new French translation of the Bible. Roman Catholic scholars at this noted research center used recent manuscript discoveries such as the Dead Sea Scrolls to produce volume after volume of the French translation, with a full complement of scholarly notes. In 1956, a one-volume edition appeared with abridged notes. The *New Jerusalem Bible* is an English translation of the extensive study notes from that French work, along with a new translation of the biblical text from the Hebrew and Greek. The notes interpret Scripture in conformity with Roman Catholic dogma. The *New Jerusalem Bible* includes the Apocrypha.

King James ("Authorized") Version. Many publishers, n.d.

First published in 1611 and revised several times thereafter, this is the classic standard against which all other English versions of the Bible are measured. The KJV is still the version most widely used by Protestant Christians, even though "simplicity and clarity are not always its chief merits" (MTBS, 179). Most modern scholars reject the KJV because its translators used rather late and defective copies of the Hebrew and Greek manuscripts. Yet conservative scholars insist that "the differences [between the manuscripts used by the KJV translators and those used later] are not that great and the KJV is extremely faithful to the text then available" (STB, 50). The American Bible Society editions and *The Open Bible* (Nashville: Thomas Nelson, 1976) explain or revise the more archaic words to aid the reader, since the English language has changed considerably from the time when the KJV was first published.

---

[11]ABS published an edition of the TEV with Apocrypha in 1979.

The Message: The New Testament in Contemporary English. Colorado Springs: NavPress, 1993.

Popular Bible teacher and author Eugene H. Peterson has written this easy-to-read paraphrase of the New Testament. The Scripture text flows as a story narrative with dialogue and simple descriptive details to help us visualize the events of New Testament times. "The goal is not to render a word-for-word conversion of Greek into English," Dr. Peterson writes, "but rather to convert the tone, the rhythm, the events, the ideas, into the way we actually think and speak" (p. 7).

New Living Translation. Wheaton: Tyndale House, 1996.

This project started when Kenneth Taylor, an editor at Moody Press, began paraphrasing portions of the New Testament from the ASV into simple English for his children. Eventually, Taylor founded Tyndale House to publish his work as he continued paraphrasing the Bible. The first edition of Taylor's paraphrase, entitled *Living Bible,* was such a loose paraphrase that it often departed from the meaning of the original. Skilled translators reviewed Taylor's work to produce this new edition. It does rectify the worst problems of the *Living Bible* and adheres more closely to the meaning of the original biblical text.

New American Bible: Standard Edition. Collegeville, MN: Liturgical Press, 1988.

This is the climax of nearly five decades of work that began in 1941, when the Confraternity of Christian Doctrine sponsored a new translation of the New Testament by the Catholic Biblical Association of America. They originally worked from the Latin Vulgate version. The translators then returned to the Hebrew and Greek texts to produce a completely new version in 1970. A few Protestant translators and editors collaborated on that first edition of the NAB, but the text bore a distinctly Roman Catholic orientation. The new 1988 edition brought helpful clarifications at some points. (Do not confuse this with the New American Standard Bible, an evangelical Protestant work.)

New American Standard Bible. LaHabra, CA: Foundation Press, 1996-98.

Dissatisfied with the RSV, the Lockman Foundation of California began work on this independent revision of the ASV in 1959. The NASB is more of a formal-equivalence version than the RSV; it more carefully preserves the meaning of each word and phrase of the original text. For that reason, it does not read as smoothly as the Revised Standard. Cyril J. Barber and other conservative reviewers praise the NASB as "perhaps the most accurate and reliable translation presently available" (ML, 49), while more liberal reviewers believe the NRSV is a better translation overall (HBE, 259).

Revised English Bible. Oxford and Cambridge: Oxford and Cambridge University Presses, 1989.

The Church of England, the Church of Scotland, and other major church groups in the British Isles jointly sponsored this translation project, which was intended to be an authoritative revision to use alongside the KJV. The translators used the Masoretic Text of the Old Testament and eclectic texts of the New Testament; they strived for a dynamic-equivalence version. However, they frequently used British expressions that can be difficult for American readers to grasp. For this reason, the REB is seldom used in the United States.

New International Version. Grand Rapids: Zondervan, 1990.

The New York Bible Society sponsored this new translation, using newer critical editions of the Hebrew and Greek manuscripts. Most of the translators came from the Reformed Church in America and other Calvinist denominations. They tried to preserve the traditional sense of the text, while using the dynamic-equivalence approach. F.F. Bruce says, "The language is dignified, readable and easily understood" (HBE, 266). The NIV is an effective wedding of modern scholarship and articulate writing.

New King James Version. Nashville: Thomas Nelson, 1982.

Some Bible versions made from the older Bible manuscripts have yielded rather unorthodox readings of Scripture. Disturbed by this trend, the editors at Nelson assembled a team of conservative Bible scholars to make the *New King James Version.* This team used a *majority text** reading of the ancient manuscripts for the Old Testament—i.e., they followed the readings given by most of the Bible manuscripts, whether they were the oldest manuscripts or not. They used the *Textus Receptus* for the New Testament. Foster says, "It is an attempt to update the wording of the King James, but to retain its beauty and degree of literalness" (STB, 44).

New Revised Standard Version. Nashville: Thomas Nelson, 1989.

The National Council of the Churches of Christ ordered this revision of the ASV, using Hebrew and Greek manuscripts that were older than those available to the ASV translators in the late 1800s. However, the translators soon abandoned the idea of revising the ASV and set out to make an entirely new translation. Although the NRSV is easier to read than the ASV or the KJV, many conservative readers complain that it distorts certain doctrines of the Bible. For example, they charge that the NRSV "waters down" the messianic prophecies of the Old Testament and obscures the connection of Old Testament prophecies quoted in the New Testament. Yet the translators insist that they made their changes because of what they found in the ancient manuscripts, not because of their own theological views. This new edition issued in 1989 employs inclusive language.

The New Testament: A Translation. 2 vols., trans. William Barclay. London: Collins, 1968-69.

Barclay says, "In making this translation I have had two aims in view. The first is to try to make the New Testament intelligible to the man who is not a technical scholar.... The second was to try to make a translation which did not need a commentary to explain it" (p. 5). He seems to have achieved the first goal, because this version is easy for any layperson to understand. But to achieve the second goal, Barclay inserted his own commentary into the text. Use this version alongside a formal-equivalence version such as the NASB or NKJV to check Barclay's ideas.

New Testament in Modern English, trans. J.B. Phillips. New York: Macmillan Publishing Company, 1972.

British writer J.B. Phillips began this work by making a new version of Paul's epistles for his soldier friends in World War II. C.S.

Lewis then encouraged Phillips to translate the rest of the New Testament. "As I see it," Phillips said in his foreword, "the translator's function is to understand as fully and deeply as possible what the New Testament writers had to say and then, after a process of what might be called reflective digestion, to write it down in the language of the people of today" (p. viii). Phillips' version gives us one of the best dynamic-equivalence readings of the New Testament.

Chapter 3

Annotated and Study Bibles

Nearly every edition of every version of the Bible has some sort of study aids for the reader. They range from *cross references** (references to other Bible verses that will help you understand the meaning of a particular verse) to a full-fledged *commentary.** Bibles with such study aids are variously called "annotated Bibles," "reference Bibles," "study Bibles," and so on. For the sake of simplicity, we will survey all types of reference Bibles under two main categories:

1. *Annotated Bibles** (with cross references and a few simple notations for *alternate readings** and *textual variants**).

2. *Study Bibles** (with more elaborate notes, an introduction and outline of each Bible book, and articles to broaden your understanding of the Bible).

How Study Aids Were Added

A brief journey back into history will demonstrate how we came to have so many kinds of Bible "helps." The year is 1604. The place is Hampton Court, the residence of King James I of England. The king has assembled the leading churchmen of his realm to discuss the current state of affairs in the Church of England. Puritan leader Dr. John Reynolds of Oxford states that dissent within the church might be calmed if all the people had a standard Bible translation. As it is, they may be using the Bishops' Bible, the Geneva Bible, William Tyndale's translation, or several other English versions that can be purchased or smuggled into the country.

Richard Bancroft, Bishop of London, does not like Reynolds' idea of a new translation. "If every man's humor were followed, there would be no end of translating," he says.

But the proposal appeals to King James, who says, "I wish some special pains were taken for a uniform translation...to be read in the whole church, and none other."

Seeing that he is about to be overruled, Bishop Bancroft urges the king to ban any notes from the new translation. He explains that the Geneva Bible's *margin notes** have been highly offensive to the Anglican leaders. King James is also disturbed when Bancroft points out the Geneva Bible's note on Exodus 1:19, which says that the Hebrew midwives had a right to disobey the Egyptian king. Then Bancroft turns to 2 Chronicles 15:19, where the Geneva Bible notes that King Asa's idolatrous mother should have been executed for her beliefs. King James I surely feels the barb of that comment, since his own mother had been executed for her zealous Roman Catholic beliefs.[1] So the king stipulates that no marginal notes should be added to the new version.

Now we step forward in time to the year 1611 and enter the London shop of Robert Barker, King James' royal printer. Bound copies of the massive new Bible are stacked on a table to dry. In one corner, an apprentice leafs through one of the finished volumes and his eyes scan the printed pages, each having two columns of Scripture—and a small column of notes in the margin! How can this be?

If we peer over the apprentice's shoulder as he comes to the preface of the book, we find the answer. The preface says that the translators found it necessary to annotate passages that seemed to present "difficultie and doubtfulnesse" to the reader.[2] As successive editions of the KJV come from the press, the editors and printers will add more study aids to the margin: cross references, alternate readings, variant spellings, even an interpretative comment now and then (despite King James' distaste for them).

Taking another step forward in time to 1701, we see the royal printer's assistants rearrange their Bible printing plates to add yet another feature, a *chronology.** They are inserting a date for every major event described in the Bible, beginning with the Creation (to which they give a date of 4004 B.C.).

Most of these dates come from a set of books entitled *Annales Veteris et Novi Testamenti*, written by Archbishop James Ussher.[3] The archbishop has computed these dates by taking Christ's birth

---

[1]F.F. Bruce, ed., *History of the Bible in English*, 3rd ed. (New York: Oxford University Press, 1978), 96-97.

[2]Quoted by Frederick W. Danker, *Multipurpose Tools for Bible Study*, 2nd ed. (St. Louis: Concordia, 1966), 178.

[3]Like most scholarly works of that day, its title is in Latin. It literally means, "Annals of the Old and New Testaments."

as the year "A.D.1" and working backwards, according to the number of years that the Old Testament gives for each event of history (such as the length of a person's life or the length of Israel's Captivity). The chronology is fascinating. And since there is no copyright law in eighteenth-century Europe, other printers soon insert the chronology in their own Bible editions.

We might make several other stops on this trip through the history of Bible study aids, but for brevity's sake we will move far ahead to the summer of 1901. The place is the northern shore of Long Island, New York. Dr. Cyrus I. Scofield, pastor of the Congregational Church at East Northfield, Massachusetts, and Arno C. Gaebelein, editor of a religious paper entitled *Our Hope*, are taking a stroll along the shore this evening. It is a restful break from the week-long Bible conference that Dr. Scofield is holding at a nearby park in Sea Cliff, Long Island. There Dr. Scofield has been teaching the *dispensational** view of Bible history, focusing on the return of Christ and His *millennial** reign. Mr. Gaebelein describes the scene for us.

> It was a beautiful night. Our walk along the shore of the Sound lasted until midnight. For the first time he mentioned the plan of producing a Reference Bible, and outlined the method he had in mind. He said he had thought of it for many years and had spoken to others about it, but had not received much encouragement.... He expressed the hope that the new beginning...in Sea Cliff might open the way to bring about the publication of such a Bible with references and copious footnotes.[4]

This new reference Bible will focus attention on the prophetic teachings of Scripture. It will interpret the full sweep of Bible history, from Creation to Final Consummation, in light of the dispensational formula. Gaebelein and Scofield soon persuade several like-minded men to finance the project. They appoint seven consulting editors to help with the work. And in 1903, Dr. Scofield resigns from the East Northfield pastorate to devote more time to the task.

---

[4]Arno C. Gaebelein, *The History of the Scofield Reference Bible* (New York: Loizeaux Brothers, 1943), 47.

Finally, in 1909, the *Scofield Reference Bible* is published by Oxford University Press in New York City. It is the first modern reference Bible and it sets up a high standard of scholarship that all subsequent reference Bibles must follow. In his preface to the book, Dr. Scofield writes:

> ...What the present book does is to present the great subjects concerning which God has revealed the future, and to assemble and analyze that revelation so that any reader of the book will find himself fully introduced to these great and important themes. The final effect...is to leave the mind overwhelmingly impressed with the divine origin and authorship of these ancient oracles. Writing in widely separated ages, under wholly different circumstances,...the production of one continuous, harmoniously developed testimony is proof unanswerable that, although He employed many penmen, God alone is the Author of the prophetic testimony.[5]

If we walk into a New York City bookstore late that year to compare Scofield's reference Bible with the other Bibles then available, we are impressed by the contrast. Other Bibles have a narrow column of cross references, alternate readings, and a chronology on each page. The *Scofield Reference Bible* has that material in *center column notes.** But it also has a lengthy introduction to each book of the Bible, *footnotes** explaining difficult passages, an index to all of the introductions and footnotes, an index of proper names, an index of Bible subjects, a concordance, and a set of Bible maps.

Dr. Scofield and his colleagues have made the Bible a textbook for study. They have given the Bible reader a set of tools for delving into the great themes of Bible teaching, even if the reader does not agree with their interpretation of that teaching.

By every measure, the *Scofield Reference Bible* forms a watershed in Bible publishing. It raises the Bible buyer's expectations to a higher plane than before. Every study Bible published since then has been obliged to provide more study aids for the reader, in light of Dr. Scofield's achievement.

---

[5]Gaebelein, 55.

What Should We Expect?

Bible publishers make impressive claims for the study aids in the new editions they issue. They customarily get endorsements (signed recommendations) from leading pastors and evangelists to support their claims for a particular Bible. We occasionally find the same people stating that two different Bibles are "the best" in some respect. A well-known evangelical writer recently said that a particular study Bible was "like a Bible correspondence school course." Another said that he could preach from a certain study Bible without any prior study, because that particular edition "lays it all out for me." With such competing claims, it's hard for the layman to know what study Bible is best to use. What features should we expect in an annotated Bible or study Bible?

Annotated Bibles

Although the annotated Bible gives only the most simple notes to the text, it should furnish a practical apparatus understanding the Scripture. We should expect an annotated Bible to contain:

1. *Alternate Readings*—The editors should provide any significant alternative way of reading a certain verse. This might be: (a) a different *translation* of the verse, if its meaning is obscure; (b) a different *reading* of the verse that was added or omitted by certain ancient manuscripts; or (c) a different *interpretation* of the verse, where the English translators have departed from what the text literally says.

2. *Cross References*—Expect to find frequent references to other Bible verses about the same topic. Some annotated Bibles simply refer you to other verses that contain the same key word used in a different way. But this concordance style of cross reference will not aid study as much as a topical reference does.

3. *Book Introductions*—Even the most simple type of reference Bible should provide some introduction to each book of the Bible. It should explain something about the contents of the book, who wrote it, and what significance it has for modern readers. Some annotated Bibles gather these introductions in a separate article, rather than placing them at the start of each Bible book.

4. *A Selective Concordance*—Look for this feature at the back of the annotated Bible. The concordance is a list of important words that occur in Scripture, arranged in alphabetical order, with ref-

erences to the verses that contain each word. A *selective* concordance will list only the most important words of Scripture (perhaps a few hundred) and will show you only a few verses that contain each word. An exhaustive concordance would be too big to include in any reference Bible. So when you turn to the concordance in the back of any Bible, you can safely assume it is a selective concordance. See Chapter 5 for instructions on how to use a concordance.

While some Bibles contain a chronology of Bible events, do not expect to find one in every reference Bible. Bible scholars now know that we cannot fix dates for most Bible events, even using Archbishop Ussher's simple method.

Ussher's chronology assumed that the Bible gives all of its dates in consecutive order, without any overlapping. But other historical records from the same period do not follow this pattern. They leave gaps in family records, they drop out events that seemed less important, and they fail to mention chronological overlaps between people's lives. Donald J. Wiseman notes that several archaeological finds do not jibe with Ussher's dates.[6] For example, the Flood evidence unearthed by Sir Leonard Woolley at Ur is older than Ussher's Flood date of 2300 B.C. Also, the artifacts from ancient sites such as Jericho are much older than Ussher's theoretical Creation date of 4004 B.C.

Modern archaeologists use some ingenious methods to assign dates to the artifacts they find, yet even these methods are not precise enough to give us reliable calendar dates. Most reference Bibles no longer carry Ussher's chronology, but they can provide nothing completely reliable to replace it.

Study Bibles

Study Bibles offer more in-depth interpretative notes, along with articles, tables, and charts that help you understand the Scriptures as we have them today. In addition to the four features that we find in an annotated Bible, a good study Bible also contains the following:

1. *In-Depth Introductions*—The study Bible should give you an

---

[6]Donald J. Wiseman, "The Chronology of the Bible," *The Holman Study Bible* (Philadelphia: A.J. Holman. 1962), 1215.

introduction to each book of the Bible. It should describe not only the theme of the book but also (a) the author, (b) the approximate date it was written, (c) the place and occasion of its writing, and (d) to whom the book may have been addressed.

2. *Outlines of the Books*—The study Bible should sketch the major themes of each book and show in outline how each passage relates to the major themes. This is especially important for books of complicated structure, such as Paul's epistles.

3. *Interpretative Notes*—The study Bible should provide some notes about the significance of certain passages. Due to space limitations, a study Bible cannot give a full-fledged commentary on the Scriptures, dissecting every verse. But it should emphasize the meaning of key verses to help you comprehend the central message.

4. *An Article on Archaeology*—Over the past two centuries, the science of archaeology has transformed our understanding of the Bible. The discoveries of archaeologists have a significant impact on what Bible editors say in their introductions and interpretative notes. So the editors of your study Bible should provide at least one supplemental article to explain how archaeology has influenced their work.

5. *An Article on Bible Texts and Transmission*—By "Bible texts," we mean the ancient Hebrew and Greek texts of Scripture. By "transmission," we mean the way in which ancient texts were copied and edited as the ancient scribes relayed ("transmitted") them to us. Knowing about this process helps us understand why we have so many textual variants.

6. *A Chart of Weights, Measures, and Money*—The people who lived in Bible times did not use the meter, the mile, the hour, the dollar, or other standards of measurement that are commonly used today. They had archaic units such as the ephah, the shekel, and the league. Your Bible editors should provide charts to translate these foreign units of measurement into terms you can understand.[7]

---

[7]Sometimes a Bible version attempts to make this conversion for us, as when the New Living Translation inserts modern money equivalents into the parable of the ungrateful servant (Matt. 18:24, 28). The problem with this approach is that our monetary values change with inflation, making the comment obsolete in just a few years. It's easier for the publisher to update the conversion charts, rather than revise the Scripture translation each time the book is reprinted.

7. *A Topical Index*—This feature differs from a concordance. While a concordance lists the specific words that appear in the Scriptures, the topical index lists general topics you might wish to study, although the actual word for that topic may not appear in the Scriptures. For example, the word *abortion* does not appear in the KJV, but the topic is discussed. So a topical index to the KJV might list the term *abortion* with a few key verses on that topic. The same might be true of *depravity, fanaticism, incarnation,* and many other topics of interest. In some study Bibles, this feature is entitled a "cyclopedic index" or an "encyclopedic index" because it also provides a brief description or definition of each topic.

8. *An Index of Proper Names*—Selective concordances that appear in annotated Bibles seldom include the names of Bible people, so you cannot use them to find the sections of Scripture that pertain to a certain person. You need an index of names—an alphabetical list with one or more Scripture references for each name. A good study Bible will contain one. Some Bible editors combine the listings of people's names and place names. Other editors give only one or the other. Some give all the proper names, while others give only a selected list. Some publish this index as a separate section, while others incorporate it into their topical index. Examine the study Bible carefully to find this feature and determine how thorough it is. The index of proper names is a valuable tool to have.

Each study Bible has its own unique features, any of which might lead you to choose one study Bible over the rest. But the eight features listed above are basic aids that should be found in any study Bible.

Buying a Reference Bible

As we noted in the previous chapter, the Bible version itself will be a key factor in your choice of a reference Bible. Here we've seen that specific study tools also will influence your decision. Consider a couple of other factors as well:

1. Notice the theological stance of the editor(s). Some study Bibles were edited by a committee of scholars from a broad range of theological backgrounds (e.g., the *Holman Study Bible*). A committee is less likely to use the study Bible as a vehicle to convey a particular set of doctrines. However, a committee may equivo-

cate on sensitive issues such as the Virgin Birth or the divine inspiration of Scripture, in order to satisfy the majority on their committee.

At the other end of the spectrum are study Bibles edited by one scholar or by a few scholars from the same school of thought (e.g., the *Scofield Reference Bible* and Walter Martin's *Cult Reference Bible*). Their position on certain issues of doctrine will be clear. If you happen to agree with that point of view, you will be quite happy with such a book. But this type of study Bible may not suggest other points of view, and it may pass over some important issues.

Generally, it's better to select a study Bible edited by a committee of scholars from a fairly wide spectrum of theological backgrounds, scholars who agree on the basic tenets of Christian doctrine. The *Open Bible* and the *Ryrie Study Bible* are two conservative, evangelical study Bibles of this type.

2. Remember that more study aids do not necessarily make a better Bible. A new Christian may eagerly compare several study Bibles at the bookstore counter, then choose the one with the most sophisticated study apparatus because he thinks he needs all the "helps" he can get. Then he tries to use the Bible and is disappointed. The "helps" are so complicated and clumsy that the budding Bible student gets frustrated, puts the Bible on the shelf, and forgets it. Usually, a few easy-to-use aids will assist your Bible study more than an elaborate system of aids.

How to Use "Helps"

Let's assume that you have chosen an annotated or study Bible. How should you use it, in order to get the most from its system of "helps"?

Each Bible has its own unique features, so take time to read the publisher's preface and/or introduction. The editor(s) will describe the special features of this book and tell why they were included. You may find suggestions here for a method of study, drawing on each of the aids that are available. Sometimes a Bible publisher will furnish a separate booklet to describe these features in fuller detail and to explain how you can use them all. At any rate, pay careful attention to the "front matter" in your reference Bible;

Figure 7–Alternate Readings from the New International Version

Type of Alternate	Scripture Passage	Footnote
Different Translation	Jesus replied, "Friend, do what you came for" (Matt. 26:50).	Or, *"Friend, why have you come?"*
	"You believe at last!" Jesus answered (John 16:31).	Or, *"Do you now believe?"*

These two examples show that even a short Greek phrase can be difficult to translate. When the translators have some doubt about the exact meaning, they put the most likely translation in the Scripture text itself and give an alternate in a note.

Type of Alternate	Scripture Passage	Footnote
Different Reading (from an ancient manuscript)	But Jesus turned and rebuked them… (Luke 9:55).	Some MSS* add, *And he said, "You do not know what kind of spirit you are of, for the Son of Man did not come to destroy men's lives, but to save them."*
	He appointed twelve—designating them apostles—that they might be with him and that he might send them out to preach (Mark 3:14).	Some MSS omit, *designating them apostles.*

The ancient manuscripts of the Bible often disagree with one another. When they do, translators will follow the reading they consider to be the most reliable, but they may show in a note some of the alternate readings found in other manuscripts. (Note: *MSS is the abbreviation for "manuscripts.")

Type of Alternate	Scripture Passage	Footnote
Clarification (i.e., more than what the verse literally says)	While Jesus was in one of the towns, a man came along who was covered with leprosy… (Luke 5:12).	The Greek word probably designated other related diseases also.
	A second time they summoned the man who had been blind. "Give glory to God," they said… (John 9:24).	A solemn charge to tell the truth (see Joshua 7:19).

Here are examples of verses that would leave the reader with a false or misleading impression, if taken at face value. Rather than "padding" the Scripture text itself with their commentary, the translators provide an explanation in a footnote.

it will get you started on the right foot. Suggestions for using some of the common reference features are listed below:

1. *Alternate Readings*—As explained earlier, an alternate reading in the margin or footnotes may show a different translation, a different reading (from certain ancient manuscripts), or a different interpretation of the verse. Figure 7 shows some examples of alternate readings from the NIV.

Be sure to check these notes so you will get the full impact of each passage. Reread the verse, inserting or deleting the material that you find in the alternate readings. See how the alternates affect the meaning of the verse. (It's best to do this before following the cross references.)

2. *Cross references*—A cross-reference note refers us to another passage of Scripture that has the same key word or deals with the same topic as the passage at hand. Figure 8 gives you some examples, showing the sorts of information that cross references may provide. (See p. 60.)

Take time to look up cross references, especially when you are making an inductive Bible study. They may fill in some crucial gaps of information about the subject under consideration.

3. *Book Introductions*—When doing a deductive Bible study (i.e., when you are trying to discern the overall content of a Bible book or a Bible character's life), you can check your own conclusions by reading the study Bible's introduction to that Bible book. (See Figure 9, p. 61.) The introduction is like the printed program for a drama; it alerts you to the writer's purpose, themes, and secondary themes. Bible-book outlines (see Section 4 below) are also vital tools for deductive study. They describe the biblical narrative in even more detail.

Suppose you have been chosen to give the baccalaureate address for a graduating college class, so you decide to explore what the Bible says about *wisdom*. Following your Bible's cross references, you come to Ecclesiastes 2:15-16:

> So I said in my heart, "As it happens to the fool, it also happens to me; and why was I then more wise?" Then I said in my heart, "This also is vanity." For there is no more remembrance of the wise than of the fool forever, since all that now is will be forgotten in the days to come. And how does the wise man die? As the fool!

That's not a very encouraging word for young men and women who have worked hard to attain knowledge and develop wisdom! You examine the surrounding verses for some explanation of this passage, but find no help. So you turn back to your reference Bible's introduction to the Book of Ecclesiastes. There you find a statement like this:

Figure 8–Useful Cross References in a Study Bible

Scripture Passage	*Cross Reference*
The discretion of a man makes him slow to anger, And his glory is to overlook a transgression (Prov. 19:11).	So then, my beloved, let every man be swift to hear, slow to speak, slow to wrath (James 1:19). And be kind to one another, tender-hearted, forgiving one another, even as God in Christ forgave you (Eph. 4:32).

These two cross references in The Nelson Study Bible: New King James Version *take us to passages on the same topic as the key passage—i.e., the topic of anger. Neither verse in the NKJV contains the English word, anger. Nor do they use the same Hebrew word, since they are both from the New Testament. So you would not find them in a concordance, perhaps not even in a topical Bible.*

Scripture Passage	*Cross Reference*
Because the carnal mind is enmity against God; for it is not subject to the law of God, nor indeed can it be (Rom. 8:7).	Adulterers and adulteresses! Do you not know that friendship with the world is enmity with God? Whoever therefore wants to be a friend of the world makes himself an enemy of God (James 4:4). But the natural man does not receive the things of the Spirit of God, for they are foolishness to him; nor can he know them, because they are spiritually discerned (1 Cor. 2:14).

These cross references from the same study Bible clarify an enigmatic statement from Paul's Letter to the Romans. The Apostle seems to imply that God condemns certain people to remain ignorant of Him. But the cross references make clear that God does not arbitrarily expel these people from His fellowship. Wayward people choose to live in ignorance and hostility to Him.

This is the book of man "under the sun," reasoning about life; it is the best man can do, with the knowledge that there is a holy God, and that He will bring everything into judgment... [The book's] conclusions are just in declaring it "vanity," in view of judgment, to devote life to earthly things...but the

Figure 9–Book Introduction From an Annotated Bible: Job

THE BOOK OF JOB

The book of Job does not attempt to explain the mystery of suffering or to "justify the ways of God with men." It aims at probing the depths of faith in spite of suffering. The ancient folktale of a patient Job (1.1–2.13; 42.7–17; Jas. 5.11) circulated orally among oriental sages in the second millennium B.C. and was probably written down in Hebrew at the time of David and Solomon or a century later (about 1000–800 B.C.). An anonymous poet of the sixth or fifth century B.C. used it as a setting for the discussion between an impatient Job and his three friends (3.1–31.40) and the Lord's discourses from the whirlwind (38.1–42.6). A later poet contributed Elihu's speeches (32.1–37.24).

The storyteller asked, "Does [man] fear God for nought?" (1.9). The poet echoed the question, "What is the Almighty, that we should serve him? And what profit do we get if we pray to him?" (21.15). Unlike the hero of the folktale who is rewarded materially for his virtues, the Job of the poem demands justice, and his final challenge shows that he regards religion and morality as man's claim for happiness (29.1–31.40). Job renounces his defiance only after the Lord asks, "Will you condemn me that you may be justified?" (40.8). Job is satisfied without self-vindication by an experience of immediate communion with God, not unlike that of the great prophets: "Now my eye sees thee" (42.5).

In the poetic language of the book, God is at work in the universe, even "to bring rain on a land where no man is" (38.26), and he is aware of evil (personified by the monsters Behemoth and Leviathan, 40.15–41.34). At the same time, he cares for Job so fully that he reveals himself personally to him and shares with him the vision of his cosmic responsibilities. A God who confesses his burdens to man is a God who is profoundly involved in the destiny of man. He is not an impassive force. In the presence of holiness and creative love, virtuous man surrenders his pride in adoration. In his own way the poet conveyed a view of sin which transcends morality, the awareness of which is possible only in the context of faith.

HERE WAS A MAN IN THE LAND OF Uz, whose name was Job; and that man was blameless and upright, one who feared God, and turned away from evil. ² There were born to him seven sons and three daughters. ³ He had seven thousand sheep, three thousand camels, five hundred yoke of oxen, and five hundred she-asses, and very many servants; so that this man was the greatest of all the people of the east. ⁴ His sons used to go and hold a feast in the house of each on his day; and they would send and invite their three sisters to eat and drink with them. all; for Job said, "It may be that my sons have sinned, and cursed God in their hearts." Thus Job did continually.

6 Now there was a day when the sons of God came to present themselves before the LORD, and Satan*a* also came among them. ⁷ The LORD said to Satan, "Whence have you come?" Satan answered the LORD, "From going to and fro on the earth, and from walking up and down on it." ⁸ And the LORD said to Satan, "Have you considered my servant Job, that there is none like him on the earth, a blameless and upright man, who fears God and turns

Source: Herbert G. May and Bruce M. Metzger, eds., *The New Oxford Annotated Bible* (New York: Oxford University Press, 1973), p. 613

Figure 10–Study Bible Outlines: Romans

The Scofield Reference Bible

The Epistle, exclusive of the introduction (1.1-17), is in seven parts:
I.   The whole world guilty before God, 1.18–3.20.
II. Justification through righteousness of God by faith.
     The Gospel remedy for guilt, 3.21–5.11.
III. Crucifixion with Christ
     The resurrection life of Christ, and the walk in the Spirit
     The Gospel provision for inherent sin, 5.12–8.13.
IV. The full result in blessing of the Gospel, 8.14-39.
V.   Parenthesis: The Gospel does not abolish the covenant promises to Israel, 9.1–11.36.
VI. Christian life and service, 12.1–15.33.
VII. The outflow of Christian service, 16.1-27.

Source: C.I. Scofield, ed., *The Scofield Reference Bible* **(New York: Oxford University Press, 1945), 1191.**

Spirit-Filled Life Bible

Introduction **1:1-17**
   A. Paul's identification 1:1-7
   B. Paul's desire to visit Rome 1:8-15
   C. Summary of the gospel 1:16, 17
I. All have sinned **1:18–3:20**
   A. Gentiles know of God but reject Him 1:18-32
   B. Jews have God's laws but are not righteous 2:1-29
   C. God is just to judge all men 3:1-20
II. Justification is by faith alone **3:21–5:21**
   A. God's righteousness preserved through Christ's death for us 3:21-26
   B. Justification is by faith alone 3:27-31
   C. Abraham justified by faith, not works 4:1-25
   D. Once justified by faith, we triumph even in sufferings 5:1-11
   E. We gained death through Adam's sin, but eternal life through Christ's obedience . 5:12-21
III. Practicing righteousness in the Christian life **6:1–8:39**
   A. Overcoming sin in the Christian life 6:1-23
   B. We are dead to the powerless system called "law" 7:1-6
   C. The law cannot empower us to obey 7:7-25
   D. We fulfill God's righteousness by living in the power of the Spirit and according to the Spirit .. 8:1-17
   E. Longing for complete redemption 8:18-25
   F. Help and assurance in hardship 8:26-39
IV. God and Israel **9:1–11:36**
   A. Though Israel is unfaithful, God is righteous 9:1-33
   B. Israel has willingly rejected the gospel 10:1-21
   C. A remnant now remains, and someday full salvation will come to Israel 11:1-32
   D. Praise for God's infinite wisdom 11:33-36
V. Practical applications **12:1–15:13**
   A. Present yourselves as sacrifices to God 12:1, 2
   B. Use of spiritual gifts 12:3-8
   C. Relating to Christians 12:9-13
   D. Relating to unbelievers 12:14-21
   E. Relating to government 13:1-7
   F. The law of love 13:8-14
   G. Toleration and love in minor things 14:1-23
   H. Caring for each other 15:1-13
VI. Paul's own situation **15:14-33**
   A. His ministry 15:14-22
   B. His plans 15:23-33
VII. Personal greetings **16:1-24**
VIII. Benediction **16:25-27**

Source: Jack W. Hayford, ed., *Spirit-Filled Life Bible* **(Nashville: Thomas Nelson, 1991), 1686.**

The differences between these two outlines may not be apparent at first, but if you look more closely, you will see the editors' different theological views. The first study Bible is Calvinist and dispensational, while the second is Wesleyan and neo-Pentecostal. While Dr. Scofield tersely mentions "Christian life and service," Dr. Hayford gives a detailed outline of Romans 12–15 to emphasize the Christian's duty. (Note: Scofield's outline has been rearranged into a parallel pattern to make the comparison easier.)

"conclusion" (12:13) is legal, the best that man apart from redemption can do, and does not anticipate the Gospel....[8]

This puts the troublesome verses in better perspective. With this view of the book's general thrust, you get a better grasp of the meaning of this particular passage.

4. *Book Outlines*—Use these outlines especially when you are engaged in a deductive study. They clearly display the themes of the book or the key events of a character's life, giving you an overview of the subject under study.

When studying a book that is theologically complex, such as the Epistle to the Romans or 1 Corinthians, compare the outline in your Bible with another from a study Bible prepared by editors of a different theological persuasion. Such a comparison may reveal two different perspectives on the message of the book. (See Figure 10.)

5. *Interpretative Notes*—These notes may give some helpful insights, but they often present the editors' theological stance as well. They may discuss the nuances of certain words, the cultural setting of the passage, how the original audience may have understood what is being said, and so on. But when interpretative notes begin to discuss "hidden meanings" or make dogmatic pronouncements, they can become a biased commentary on the text.

Remember that these notes are merely the editors' interpretations of Scripture. They are not Scripture itself. So do not assume that an interpretative note is the final, infallible word on a given passage.

6. *Supplemental Aids*—Other features, such as the article on archaeology or the table of weights and measures, will not be vital to your Bible study every time you open the Word. Refer to them only when you need them.

Suppose that the editors' introduction to Genesis raises a question in your mind about how the Jews preserved this great book through so many centuries. So you turn to your study Bible's article on Bible texts and their transmission. Perhaps you wonder whether archaeologists have found evidence of the miraculous

---

[8]C.I. Scofield, ed., *The Scofield Reference Bible* (New York: Oxford University Press, 1945), 696.

victory won by Joshua's armies at Jericho (Josh. 6). The answer may be found in your study Bible's article on archaeology. Or perhaps you are reading about Peter's finding a four-drachma coin in the mouth of a fish (Matt. 17:24-27), and you wonder how much that coin would be worth today. Look at your study Bible's table of monetary values for the answer.

These supplemental aids can help to bring the Scriptures to life. Use these aids and the other features of your reference Bible as tools to uncover what God's Word is saying to you today.

ANNOTATED BIBLIOGRAPHY

The annotated and study Bibles listed below are arranged alphabetically by the editor's surname, or by title if the editor's name is not given. The phrase, "red-letter edition," means that the words of Christ are printed in red.

Good News Bible: Catholic Study Edition. Nashville: Thomas Nelson, 1979.

This Roman Catholic work has only minimal study aids. The introductions to the books are sketchy, the footnotes are sparse, and there are relatively few subheadings to show the themes of the text. The editors have grouped the apocryphal books together between the Testaments, which is not the traditional Catholic order. Despite these weaknesses, the work does supply some useful study aids for the Good News Bible and offers Catholic readers a simple, easy-to-use reference Bible.

Hayford, Jack W., general ed. *Spirit-Filled Life Bible.* Nashville: Nelson, 1991.

Described by Pastor Hayford as "a study Bible integrating the Pentecostal-Charismatic viewpoint" (p. v), this book contains study notes from dozens of the best-known charismatic church leaders. Yet it treats potentially controversial passages with balance and clarity, avoiding any party spirit. (See for example its treatment of Acts 2:1-13 and James 5:13-15.) Using the NKJV text, the *Spirit-Filled Life Bible* contains rich doctrinal insight in the word studies and margin notes. Any Christian would benefit from the use of this book.

Keefauver, Larry, ed. *Holy Spirit Encounter Bible*. Orlando, FL: Creation House, 1997.

Using the text of the New Living Translation, the *Holy Spirit Encounter Bible* guides the reader on a study of the Holy Spirit's work throughout the Bible. Full-page study guides entitled, "Holy Spirit Encounters," explain the various aspects of the Spirit's ministry at crucial points of biblical history. Vignetted study notes called "Holy Spirit Encounter Moments" give a Bible teacher pointed questions for those who are reading a given passage. Cross references and footnotes are meager. However, charismatic readers will enjoy the emphasis of the teaching notes. One unique feature is the compilation of passages entitled, "The Holy Spirit throughout the Bible."

May, Herbert G., and Bruce M. Metzger, eds. *The New Oxford Annotated Bible*. New York: Oxford University Press, 1991.

The editors aptly call this an "annotated Bible" rather than a study Bible, because they have kept the interpretative notes and other study aids to a minimum. They use the New Revised Standard Version of 1989. They provide a brief introduction to each book of the Bible, commenting on its author, title, date, contents, and literary genre. They usually reflect a liberal view of *literary criticism** in these introductions. (See for example the introductions to Genesis, Isaiah, and the epistles of Peter). The editors also follow the practice of putting certain portions of Scripture in small italic footnotes because they doubt the authenticity of these passages. (Notice Acts 8:37 and 1 Pet. 5:2.) *The New Oxford Annotated Bible* groups the books of the Apocrypha at the end of the Bible. The editors use brief footnotes to give alternate readings, cross reference, and an outline of the contents. This annotated Bible carries the *nihil obstat** and *imprimatur** of the Roman Catholic Church.

Meeks, Wayne, ed. *The HarperCollins Study Bible: New Revised Standard Version*. New York: Harper, 1997.

Designed to serve the daily study needs of readers who wish to have the results of the modern biblical scholarship close at hand, The *HarperCollins Study Bible* uses the NRSV text for the entire Bible, including the apocrypha and Deuterocanonical books. The footnotes give the reader clear insight into biblical history and theology. The introductions to various Bible books tend to explore academic textual issues to a greater extent than most pastors or lay readers would need. Christians in mainline denominations will use this study Bible with profit.

Nave, Orville J., and Anna Semans Nave. *Nave's Study Bible*. Ada, MI: Baker Books, 1997.[9]

This is one of the oldest study Bibles still in print. Developed in the late 1800s, it uses the KJV text with alternate readings from the RV. *Nave's Study Bible* has generous cross references in the margin and links Old Testament messianic prophecies with their fulfillment in the New Testament. Nave's footnotes are very brief. The dictionary-concordance is keyed to refer back to the footnotes. Nave includes the Ussher chronology, but the publishers have inserted question marks after many of the dates. Although this work is a classic, its underlying research is too out-of-date for the book to be of much use.

Rademacher, Earl D., Ronald B. Allen and H. Wayne House, eds. *The Nelson Study Bible*. Nashville: Thomas Nelson, 1997.

Bringing together an impressive team of conservative Bible scholars from Baptist and Presbyterian backgrounds, *Nelson's Study Bible* provides a full set of study tools for the NKJV. Features include extensive study notes, "Word Focus" sidebar articles on key biblical terms, and clear maps strategically located in the text. The crisp, modern page design makes even the footnotes easy to read. The 193-page concordance is more complete than one normally finds in a study Bible. *Nelson's Study Bible* should be considered one of the most useful study Bibles published in recent years.

Ryrie, Charles C., ed. *The Ryrie Study Bible*. Chicago: Moody Press, 1979.

Dr. Ryrie of Dallas Theological Seminary takes a solidly conservative position in the study notes of this Bible. For example, in his introductory notes, he makes a strong defense of Moses'

---

[9]Also available from (Nashville: Broadman & Holman Publishers, 1978) and (Nashville: Thomas Nelson, 1997).

authorship of the Pentateuch and Isaiah's authorship of the entire Book of Isaiah. He gives extensive footnotes and detailed outlines of the Bible books. His comments on prophecy are strongly dispensational and *premillennial.** An interesting feature is Dr. Ryrie's "Synopsis of Bible Doctrine" in the back of the book—an outline of key Bible doctrines presented in systematic style with Scripture references. This study Bible is available with the KJV or NASB text and in red-letter editions.

Scofield, C.I., ed. *The New Scofield Reference Bible.* New York: Oxford University Press, 1967.

The editorial committee for this revised edition (headed by E. Schuyler English) made several changes in Scofield's work to make it more useful to modern readers. They revised the archaic spellings of the KJV text at many points. They expanded the introduction to each Bible book to discuss its author and date and to give a brief outline. They simplified the numbering system for the footnotes. They expanded the footnotes when necessary, to deal with questions about Scofield's interpretation of prophecy. The revisers also removed Ussher's chronology from the center column, "because of the lack of evidence on which to fix dates" (p. vi). However, they were careful to preserve and explain Scofield's comments on the dispensations of history. Oxford has also reissued the original 1917 edition.

Thompson, F.C., ed. *The New Chain-Reference Bible.* Indianapolis: B.B. Kirkbride Bible Company, 1982.

This ingenious work combines the features of a topical Bible and a simple cross reference Bible. Instead of referring you to a few selected cross references on a particular topic, the editor sends you to a "chain" of marginal cross references on the topic. Notes along the lefthand margin give the "pilot reference"—the Scripture verse where a cross reference "chain" on that topic begins. Notes along the right-hand margin give the "forward reference"—the verse that is the next link in a "chain" you might be following. In the back of the Bible, the editor gives a "Text Cyclopedia," where he has assembled each entire chain of references and listed the chains by topic in alphabetical order (much like a topical Bible). Thompson's original Chain Reference Bible used the KJV, but an edition using the NIV was published by Zondervan in 1983 and others using new translations are likely to follow.

Topical Chain Study Bible. Nashville: Thomas Nelson, 1982.

Patterned after F.C. Thompson's *Chain-Reference Bible*, this volume uses color-coded blocks to identify major biblical themes and a system of number codes to lead you from one topic to another. Two advantages make this study Bible preferable to Thompson's: It uses the 1971 edition of the NASB text (which is easier than the KJV for modern readers to comprehend) and the type is set in a large, single-column format.

Chapter 4

Topical Bibles

In the summer of 1969, I went from door to door, selling Bibles and Bible reference books in Mount Holly, North Carolina. One of the most popular books I sold was *Nave's Topical Bible*. As I recall, the sales pitch that we used for Nave's went something like this:

"Mrs. Jones, did you realize the Bible that Billy Graham holds when he preaches on TV is a *Nave's Topical Bible*?"[1]

That statement got people's attention. Aside from the fact that they respected Billy Graham as an evangelist, folks wanted to know why anyone would use a topical Bible instead of a regular Bible. They were sure to ask, "What's a topical Bible?" And then I would tell them.

A regular Bible presents the Scriptures in traditional *canonical** order, beginning with Genesis and ending with the Book of Revelation. A topical Bible presents the Scriptures in topical order. That is to say, a topical Bible alphabetically lists several hundred Bible-related topics, quoting the Scriptures related to each topic. Figure 11 shows a sample entry from Nave's for the topic, "Seven." Notice that it cites a wide range of Scriptures connected with that topic. Also notice that the topical Bible does not print all of the Scripture references in full; it quotes only the most significant ones and gives references for the rest.

(One verse might relate to a half-dozen topics, so it is impractical for the topical Bible to print it in full every time. If the editors did that, the topical Bible would be several times the size of a regular Bible. It would occupy several volumes!)

A topical Bible can be a great time-saver for any Bible student. Instead of poring over cross-references or concordances for hours on end, you can have at your fingertips the pertinent passages on

---

[1] I do not know how the company determined that Billy Graham preached from *Nave's Topical Bible*. After hearing him quote translations other than the KJV (which Nave's uses), I am sure he does not always preach from Nave's. But the dust jackets on two editions of Nave's carry Dr. Graham's statement that, "outside of the Bible, this is the book I depend on more than any other."

Figure 11–Topical Bible Entry: "Seven"

SEVEN. Interesting facts concerning the number. **DAYS:** Week consists of, Gen. 2:3; Ex. 20:11; Deut. 5:13, 14. Noah in the ark before the flood, Gen. 4:10; remains in the ark after sending forth the dove, Gen. 8:10, 12. Mourning for Jacob lasted, Gen. 50:10; of Job, Job 2:13. The plague of bloody waters in Egypt lasted, Ex. 7:25. The Israelites compassed Jericho, Josh. 6:4. The passover lasted, Ex. 12:15. Saul directed by Samuel to tarry at Gilgal, awaiting the prophet's command, 1 Sam. 10:8; 13:8. The elders of Jabesh-gilead ask for a truce of, 1 Sam. 11:3. Dedication of the temple lasted double, 1 Kin. 8:65. Ezekiel sits by the river Chebar in astonishment, Ezek. 3:15. The feast of tabernacles lasted, Lev. 23:34, 42. Consecration of priests and altars lasted, Ex. 29:30, 35. Ezek. 43:25, 26. Defilements lasted, Lev. 12:2; 13:4. Fasts of, 1 Sam. 31:13; 2 Sam. 12:16; 18:22. The firstborn of flocks and sheep shall remain with mother, before being offered, Ex. 22:30. The feast of Ahasuerus continued, Esth. 1:5. Paul tarries at Tyre, Acts 21:4; at Puteoli, Acts 28:14.

Source: Orville J. Nave, ed., Nave's Topical Bible *(Nashville: Thomas Nelson, 1979), 1264.*

just about any Bible topic you would like to study. In spite of its great usefulness, many people have never heard of the topical Bible. Why is this?

The reason lies in history. The classics in this field were compiled in the late 1800s, when revivals brought to the Lord thousands of new converts who knew very little about the Bible. Christian leaders such as Orville J. Nave (a chaplain in the Civil War) and R.A. Torrey (an evangelist and pastor) worked with these new converts every day and knew firsthand their acute need for easy-to-use Bible study aids. Concordances were bulky, expensive, and hard for new converts to use. They needed something that would quickly guide them to Scriptures that spoke to their needs. So the idea of a topical Bible was born.[2]

The demand for topical Bibles slackened when study Bibles began to appear around 1900. The study Bibles provided their own system of topical references in the margin notes, a topical index, or both. Many laypeople found this study apparatus was all they needed, so the topical Bibles fell in popularity. Some Christian

[2]While browsing the library stacks at Vanderbilt Divinity School for topical Bibles, I found at least a dozen books of this sort—all published in the late 1800s.

bookstores no longer stock topical Bibles at all; a customer must place a special order to get one.

A Multipurpose Tool

The topical Bible can be a versatile Bible study tool. Here are a few of the ways you might use one in your study:

1. *To review all key Scriptures on a certain Bible topic.* This is the chief purpose of a topical Bible and the way Bible students most often use it. Perhaps you want to study the issue of God's influence upon national affairs. Figure 12 shows what you might find under the topic, "Nation." These Scriptures show how God influenced the history of Israel, how He punished the nation for its sins, how corrupt rulers affected the nation's relationship with God, how the people prayed for God's blessing upon the nation, and so on.

Notice that the entry gives cross-references to other related topics, such as "Sin, National"; "Government"; "King"; and "Rulers." If you check these entries, you will find even more scriptural teaching on the subject. These entries may suggest other topics such as "Patriotism" or "Politics," where you find even more information.

Figure 12–Topical Bible Entry, "Nation"

NATION. Sins of, Isa. 30:1, 2. Chastised, Isa. 14:26, 27; Jer. 5:29; 18:6-10; 25:12-33; Ezek. 2:3-5; 39:23, 24; Dan. 7:9-12; 9:3-16; Hos. 7:12; Joel 1:1-20; Amos 9:9; Zeph. 3:6, 8. Perish, Psa. 9:17; Isa. 60:12.

National adversity, prayer in, Judg. 21:2-4; 2 Chr. 7:13,14; Psa. 74; Joel 2:12; lamented, Ezra 9; Neh. 1:4-11; Jer. 6:14; 8:11, 20, 21; 9:1, 2. See SIN, NATIONAL.

Prayer for, Psa. 85:1-7; Lam. 2:20-22; 5; Dan. 9:3-21.

Involved in sins of rulers, Gen. 20:4, 9; 2 Sam. 24:10-17; 1 Chr. 21:7-17; of other individuals, as Achan, Josh. 7:1, 11-26.

Peace of, Job 34:29; Psa. 33:12; 89:15-18. Promises of peace to, Lev. 26:6; 1 Kin. 2:33; 2 Kin. 20:19; 1 Chr. 22:9; Psa. 29:11; 46:9; 72:3, 7; 128:6; Isa. 2:4; 14:4-7; 60:17, 18; 65:25; Jer. 30:10; 50:34; Ezek. 34:25-28; Hos. 2:18; Mic. 4:3,4; Zech. 1:11; 3:10; 8:4, 5; 9:10; 14:11. Prayer for peace, Jer. 29:7; 1 Tim. 2:1, 2. Peace given by God, Josh. 21:44; 1 Chr. 22:18; 23:25; Psa. 147:13, 14; Eccl. 3:8; Isa. 45:7. Instances of national peace, Josh. 14:15; Judg. 3:11, 30; 1 Kin. 4:24, 25. See WAR.

Righteousness exalteth, Prov. 14:34.

See GOVERNMENT; KING; RULERS.

Source: Orville J. Nave, ed., Nave's Topical Bible *(Nashville: Thomas Nelson, 1979), 896.*

Figure 13–Topical Bible Entry, "Andrew"

ANDREW. An apostle. A fisherman, Matt. 4:18. Of Bethsaida, John 1:44. A disciple of John, John 1:40. Finds Peter, his brother, and brings him to Jesus, John 1:40-42. Call of, Matt. 4:18; Mark 1:16. His name appears in the list of the apostles in Matt. 10:2; Mark 3:18; Luke 6:14. Asks the Master privately about the destruction of the temple, Mark 13:3, 4. Tells Jesus of the Greeks who sought to see him, John 12:20-22. Reports the number of loaves at the feeding of the five thousand, John 6:8. Meets with the disciples after the Lord's ascension, Acts 1:13.

Source: Orville J. Nave, ed., Nave's Topical Bible *(Nashville: Thomas Nelson, 1979), 59.*

When making a topical study like this, I jot down on a sheet of paper all of the Scripture references that interest me. Then I look up the references that the topical Bible did not quote in full, writing those passages on another sheet of paper. When I'm finished, I have several sheets of paper with Scripture passages pertaining to the topic I am studying. I place these beside the passages already quoted in the topical Bible, so that I can review what the Bible says about that topic. Often this is how I begin my research for a sermon, a Sunday school lesson, or an article. The topical study brings together several related Scriptures and provides perspective on what the entire Word of God says about the topic.[3]

2. *To review the key events of a Bible character's life.* The better topical Bibles have proper-name entries for most of the men and women mentioned in Scripture. Figure 13 shows an entry for "Andrew." The entry begins with Scriptures that identify who Andrew was and describe his background. Then the topical Bible gives a list of Scriptures that describe the important events of Andrew's life in chronological sequence.

Notice the advantage of using a topical Bible rather than a concordance when researching Bible characters. A concordance gives you only the passages that contain the person's name, but the topical Bible includes every passage that refers to the person, including verses that do not contain the person's actual name. Fur-

---

[3]*Nave's Topical Bible* and a few others are available on CD-ROM, in case you prefer to do your research by computer.

thermore, a concordance lists these passages in canonical sequence, the order in which they occur in the books of the Bible. Such a list does not show you the *time sequence* in which the events occurred, but the topical Bible's list of references does this. For these reasons, the topical Bible's arrangement can be more useful for biographical study.

3. *To find Scriptures that interpret the significance of a Bible character.* Were we to study only the events of a Bible person's life, we might miss the reason why Scripture describes the person. The topical Bible gives Scripture texts that both narrate the person's life and interpret the meaning of that life. As an example, here are some of the subheadings listed under "David" in *Nave's Topical Bible*:[4]

> Devoutness of...
>
> Justice in the Administration of...
>
> Discreetness of...
>
> Meekness of...
>
> Merciful...
>
> David as Musician...
>
> Poet...
>
> Prophet...
>
> Type of Christ...
>
> Jesus Called Son of...
>
> Prophecies Concerning Him and His Kingdom...

4. *To find examples of how a scriptural teaching is applied.* A topical Bible not only gives the passages that refer to a teaching (e.g., "Obedience"), but also a list of passages that show how various persons in the Bible applied or exemplified that teaching. Here is a list of the Scripture references under "Obedience to God—Exemplified" in *The New Topical Text Book*.[5]

> *Noah*, Gen. 6:22.
>
> *Abram*, Gen. 12:1-4, with Heb. 11:8, Gen. 22:3, 12.
>
> *Israelites*, Exod. 12:28, Exod. 24:7.

---

[4]Orville J. Nave, ed. *Nave's Topical Bible* (Nashville: Thomas Nelson, 1979), 278.

[5]R.A. Torrey, *The New Topical Text Book*, rev. ed. (Old Tappan, NJ: Fleming H. Revell, 1897), 185.

Caleb, Num. 32:12.

Asa, 1 Kings 5:11.

Elijah, 1 Kings 17:5.

Hezekiah, 2 Kings 18:6.

Josiah, 2 Kings 22:2.

David, Psa. 119:106.

Zerubbabel, Hag. 1:12.

Joseph, Matt. 1:24.

Wise Men, Matt. 2:12.

Zacharias, Luke 1:6.

Paul, Acts 26:19.

Saints of Rome, Rom. 16:19.

Obviously, these are not all of the obedient people mentioned in Scripture. However, the topical list gives us a variety of men and women as illustrations of those who have obeyed God.

5. *To make a systematic study of Bible doctrine.* A topical Bible leads you through the most sophisticated teachings of God's Word in an organized, systematic way. It's like a teaching outline. In fact, some pastors and Sunday school teachers lift their outlines from a topical Bible when they teach doctrinal subjects. Here is a good example of the systematic teaching format, again drawn from *The New Topical Text Book.*[6] To save space, I have not given the Scripture references with the outline, but I have indicated the number of references in parentheses.

Creditors
> *Defined (1)*

Might Demand
> *Pledges (2)*
> *Security of Others (2)*
> *Mortgages on Property (1)*
> *Bills or Promissory Notes (1)*
> *To Return before Sunset, Garments Taken in Pledge (3)*

---

[6]Torrey, 68.

Prohibited From

Taking Millstones in Pledge (1)
Violently Selecting Pledges (1)
Exacting Usury from Brethren (2)
Exacting Debts from Brethren During Sabbatical Year (1)
Might Take Interest from Strangers (1)
Sometimes Entirely Remitted Debts (3)
Often Cruel in Exacting Debts (3)

Often Exacted Debts

By Selling the Debtor or Taking Him for a Servant (2)
By Selling the Debtor's Property (1)
By Selling the Debtor's Family (3)
By Imprisonment (2)
From the Sureties (2)
Were Often Defrauded (2)

Illustrative Of

God's Claim upon Men (3)
The Demands of the Law (1)

6. *To trace the development of a Bible doctrine.* Most topical Bibles list doctrinal Scriptures in canonical order under a given topic. This allows the reader to trace the gradual unfolding of a doctrine (e.g., "Justification") under the Old Covenant and the New. So you can see God's progressive revelation of that truth throughout Bible times.

What to Expect

Compared to the number of study Bibles now available, the selection of topical Bibles is scanty indeed. Bible publishers offer us few titles in this category. But watch for these qualities in any topical Bible you might select:

1. *An appropriate selection of topics.* While the classics such as *Nave's* cover the standard topics of Bible study (e.g., Bible doctrines, characters, places, events), some of the newer topical Bibles include rather offbeat or faddish topics to attract a prospec-

tive buyer's attention. Some of these books claim to show what the Scriptures say on topics like "Automobile," "Atomic Bomb," "Computer," or "Popular Music." While Scripture may touch on these topics in some secondary way, it does not give God's definitive Word on them. This faddish type of topic selection will distort your understanding of Scripture today and make your topical Bible obsolete tomorrow.

2. *Adequately broad coverage of topics.* Some topical Bibles omit topics that are important to any Bible student. To produce a small, inexpensive topical Bible, the editors may eliminate hundreds of important Bible topics or give only a few references for the topics they do list. For example, the editors of some topical Bibles have eliminated all proper names. Others have abbreviated the coverage of doctrinal topics.

So make a few spot checks on a topical Bible's coverage before purchasing it. For example, see if it includes entries for important Bible characters such as Melchizedek, Josiah, Simeon, and Stephen. Notice how many references the topical Bible gives for major doctrines such as "Redemption," "Atonement," "Justification," "Salvation," "Grace," and "Sanctification." If there are only a half dozen or so references for each one, the coverage is too superficial. Finally, thumb through the pages and look for faddish entries such as the ones mentioned earlier. If you find several of these, the editors may have used poor judgment in selecting other topics as well.

3. *Clear, understandable headings.* Space limitations do not permit any topical Bible to quote all of the Scripture passages in full. The editors must give only the references for some Scripture readings and supply brief headings to explain their content. Skillful editors will provide clear, understandable headings. However, some editors provide headings that confuse or mislead. Consider these two examples:

"*Priests*—Emoluments of…"

"*Reprobacy*…See *Obduracy.*"

A topical Bible must have "handles" that are easy for the common reader to grasp, if it is to be a useful tool for Bible study.

ANNOTATED BIBLIOGRAPHY

This list of topical Bibles does not include books of Bible quotations,[7] even though such books also may be organized topically. Books of Bible quotations contain a more arbitrary selection of Scripture passages, so they may not have the Bible's most definitive statements on a given subject. The books listed here provide a more thorough and systematic treatment of Scripture, in topical form.

Holman Topical Concordance. Philadelphia: A.J. Holman, 1979.

This is a revision of *The New Topical Text Book*, a favorite turn-of-the-century topical Bible by R.A. Torrey. The basic change is that, while *The New Topical Text Book* arranged subheadings in a philosophically systematic order, the *Holman Topical Concordance* arranges them in alphabetical order. The Holman editors have also added several new topics of interest to modern readers.

Joy, Charles R., ed. *Harper's Topical Concordance*, rev. ed. New York: Harper, 1976.

According to the editor, this book contains 2,775 topics with about 33,200 Scripture passages. All of the Scripture texts are printed in full, using small type. Nonetheless, it is rather easy to find subjects in this book because the editor supplies a generous number of cross-references between topics. The book includes appropriate readings for special days—e.g., Bible readings for Lincoln's Birthday, Father's Day, Ash Wednesday, and so on. The book also includes several headings that were of special interest in the late 1950s when the book was first published, such as "(racial) Integration" and "Segregation."

Monser, Harold E., A.T. Robertson, and R.A. Torrey. *Topical Index and Digest of the Bible.* Ada, MI: Baker, 1983.

First published in 1914, Monser's *Topical Index and Digest* was expanded by Baker Books to include topical references from older topical Bibles by R.A. Torrey and A.T. Robertson. The most interesting feature of this work is its expanded treatment of the persons

---

[7]A classic book of Bible quotations is Jo Petty's *Apples of Gold* (Norwalk, CT: C.R. Gibson, 1965).

of the Bible. For example, under *Jesus Christ* is a listing of all of Jesus' key teachings on topics such as *False Teachers, Tribulation*, and *Works.* Thus, Monser's book is a handy resource for studying important Bible characters.

Nave, Orville J., ed. *Nave's Topical Bible*. Nashville: Thomas Nelson, 1979.[8]

The editor began work on this book during the Civil War, while he served as an army chaplain. "The quiet of army garrisons, apart from the rush and distraction of dense communities, has been favorable to its careful preparation," he wrote (p. 5). He used the KJV, with occasional alternate readings from the RV, arranged under more than twenty thousand topics. Nave included all of the proper names found in the Bible. *Nave's Topical Bible* is the standard in this field. It does not include some topics of modern interest, such as "Homosexuality" (see "Affections"), and some of its topic headings can mislead modern readers (e.g., "Infidelity" contains only Scriptures about infidelity to God, not marital infidelity). However, it is still the most complete and useful listing of Scripture topics now available.

---

[8]Also available with NIV text from John R. Kohlenberger III, ed., *Zondervan's NIV Nave's Topical Bible* (Grand Rapids: Zondervan, 1992).

Chapter 5

Concordances

Suppose you are talking with a friend about how to receive the eternal life that Jesus Christ offers. You are reading Scripture passages that you feel will be of special help. You vaguely recall a verse that says, "...He is faithful and just to forgive us our sins, and to cleanse us from all unrighteousness." But you can't remember the rest of the verse and you're not sure where it is located. How do you find this verse in the Bible?

One way would be to search through the Bible, page by page. There are about thirty-one thousand verses, so this approach would take quite a bit of time.

A better way would be to find the verse with the help of a *concordance.** You can open this book and find a key word that you remember from the passage (perhaps the word *forgive*) in the concordance's alphabetical list. Under that word, you find references to all the verses of the Bible that contain it. Beginning with the Book of Genesis, the list takes you to each Bible verse containing the word, *forgive*. Soon you come across a line that says:

I Jo. 1.9 he is faithful and just to forgive us...[1]

You turn to 1 John 1:9 and read the verse in full. This is the way that thousands of Bible students use their concordances every day.

A concordance is a most helpful reference book in your Bible study library. You can use it to locate a Bible verse that you need, to compare the various ways a Greek or Hebrew word is translated, or to examine the biblical development of an important idea or doctrine, or to do several other types of study. The concordance is a pathfinder with which you should be well acquainted.

---

[1]Robert Young, ed., *Young's Analytical Concordance to the Bible* (Nashville: Thomas Nelson, 1980), 367.

An Interesting History

Bible concordances were being published long before the King James Version came off the press. In fact, the first Bible concordance was compiled before the Bible had been divided into verses! However, the original purpose of the Bible concordance was not to help people locate elusive verses.

Cardinal Hugo de Santo Care wished to compare similar Scripture passages from the Latin Vulgate. So he enlisted the help of several hundred monks to compile "parallels" (Latin, *concordant*)—that is, lists of Scripture passages that contained the same or similar words. The first *concordant* were published in 1230.[2]

For easy reference, these monks used the Bible chapter divisions that had been made by Stephen Langton, the late Archbishop of Canterbury. Cardinal Hugo further divided each chapter into seven equal parts and each of these was divided into twenty-four subsections, corresponding to the twenty-four letters of the Latin alphabet. The monks did not copy the actual Scripture passages; they just made a list of these references. Here is an example of what they might have listed under the phrase, "Verily, I say unto you":

> Mathias V • III • F[3]
> Mathias V • IV • T
> Mathias VI • I • E
> Mathias VI • I • N

Using this list of "parallels" was easier than combing the entire New Testament to find the "Verily" passages of Jesus. Yet without the quoted Scripture passages themselves, the *concordant* were of limited usefulness. Three Dominican friars in England rectified this problem by 1252, by quoting brief phrases of the Scripture passages in Cardinal Hugo's list. (This was still nearly three hundred years before the Bible was divided into verses![4])

Over the following years, Bible scholars compiled similar *concordant* for the Hebrew Old Testament, the Septuagint, and the Greek New Testament. But the first English concordance was not

---

[2]Frederick W. Danker, *Multipurpose Tools for Bible Study*, 2nd ed. (St. Louis: Concordia, 1966), 1-2.

[3]This reference signified the Gospel of Matthew (Latin, *Mathias*), Chapter 5, Section III (of the seven equal divisions), Sentence "F."

[4]The Geneva Bible of 1539 was the first to use numbered verse divisions.

published until 1540, having been compiled by Thomas Gybson.[5] Gybson's concordance covered the New Testament only and it referred to passages by chapter numbers only. In 1550, John Marbeck published the first English-language concordance of the entire Bible, still without referring to verse numbers. The title of Marbeck's work is an interesting summary of the purpose that a Bible concordance had assumed by that time:

> *A Concordance,*
> *that is to say, a work wherein*
> *by the order of the letters of the A.B.C.*
> *you may readily find any word*
> *contained in the whole Bible,*
> *so often as it is there expressed or mentioned.*[6]

No longer was the concordance merely a list of parallels, like a "frequency list" (which tells the reader how often a certain word or phrase appears in the Bible, and in which books it appears). The concordance had become a ready reference tool to help Bible readers find and study the occurrences of any significant word in Scripture.

The Scottish Duo

Scottish children of the eighteenth century who lived in pious Presbyterian homes were not allowed to play sports or table games on the Sabbath. However, they were permitted to indulge in Bible word hunts. With a long strip of paper in hand, each child would scan the lines of a chosen Bible book, noting every reference to a particular word.

A lad of Aberdeen named Alexander Cruden became so obsessed with this game that he spent every spare moment making Bible word searches of his own. He worked by day as a bookseller in London, by night as a printer's proofreader. Yet he rose from bed early each morning to glean further entries for his Bible concordance. One biographer says that he completed his work in a year's time,[7] although that seems incredible.

---

[5]Danker, 9.

[6]Danker, p. 9. (I have modernized the spellings in this title to convey the sense more clearly.)

[7]Edith Olivier. *The Eccentric Life of Alexander Cruden* (London: Faber and Faber, 1934), 58.

At any rate, in 1737, Cruden published *A Complete Concordance of the Old and New Testaments.* He cited thirteen English Bible concordances that had been published up to that time, including Marbeck's; but Cruden's was the first that claimed to be "complete." Even his claim was qualified. He wrote:

> ...Though it be called in the title-page A Complete Concordance, poor sinful man can do nothing absolutely perfectly and complete, and therefore the word Complete is only to be taken in the comparative sense.[8]

Indeed, Cruden overlooked many Bible references in his concordance. He inserted some of them in the two revisions he made before his death in 1770. Even then, his concordance was not a thorough listing of all references to all the words of the Bible. It was complete, but not exhaustive.[9]

An Edinburgh bookseller named Robert Young, who had a mastery of ancient biblical languages, issued his *Analytical Concordance to the Holy Bible* in 1862. Young listed the key words alphabetically, as Cruden and earlier concordance editors had done, but he went one step further. Young listed the Scripture passages under each English word according to the Hebrew or Greek word that it translated. Figure 14 compares an entry from Cruden's concordance with the same entry from Young's concordance. Notice how Young displayed the linguistic origin of each word.

The Exhaustive Concordance

In 1890, Dr. James Strong of Drew University published his *Exhaustive Concordance of the Bible.* Here at last was a concordance that attempted to list every occurrence of every word in the KJV. This mammoth volume has gone through more than twenty-five editions, and each time the editors have added a few entries that were missed in the original effort.

Instead of dissecting in the concordance itself the Hebrew and Greek background of each word, Dr. Strong published two supplemental dictionaries of the Hebrew and Greek texts that the

---

[8]Olivier, 65.

[9]One of the sad ironies of history is that Alexander Cruden spent much of his life in insane asylums for various reasons. Yet his friends regarded him as a genius, a veritable encyclopedia of Bible knowledge.

KJV translators had used. In these dictionaries, he gave each Hebrew or Greek word a code number. Then he tagged each citation in the *Exhaustive Concordance* with the corresponding code number, to show which Hebrew or Greek word occurred in that verse. A student using the *Exhaustive Concordance* can do a Hebrew or Greek word study by following these code numbers to Strong's dictionaries. But you do not have to deal with a linguistic apparatus in the concordance itself, if you are simply interested in studying the English text.

Figure 14–Cruden's and Young's Concordances

Alexander Cruden's *Complete Concordance* (1737)

KINSMAN.

Num.	5. 8.	if the man have no k. to recompense
	27. 11.	ye shall give his inheritance to his k.
Deu.	25. †5.	her husband's next k. shall go in
	†7.	if a man like not to take his next k. wife
Ruth	2. 1.	Naomi had a k. his name was Boaz
	3. 9.	thou art a near k.
	12.	a k. nearer than I

Robert Young's Analytical Concordance (1862)

KINSMAN, (next or near)—

1. *To free, redeem,* גָּאַל *gaal.*

Num.	5.	8.	if the man have no kinsman to recompe.
	2.	20.	the man (is) near, one of our next kins.
	3.	9.	spread therefore, for thou (art) a near k.
	3.	12.	now it is true that I (am thy) near kins.
	3.	12.	howbeit there is a kinsman nearer than I

......

2. *Acquaintance,* מוֹדָע *moda*

Ruth	2.	1.	Naomi had a kinsman of her husband's

3. *Near,* קָרוֹב *qarob*

Psa. 38.	11.	My lovers...and my kinsmen stand afar

Notice that Cruden lists the Scripture references in straight canonical order, while Young divides the references according to the original Hebrew or Greek word. Young also indicates the literal meaning of each Hebrew or Greek word.

Strong's Exhaustive Concordance has become the most popular Bible concordance in the English language. Publishers have brought out other concordances keyed to the newer versions (see the Annotated Bibliography at the end of this chapter), but none of them rival the perennial popularity of Strong's.

Beyond Proof Texting

You can use a concordance to track down a Bible passage that you partially recall. Suppose you remember a fragment of a Scripture quotation and want to find the complete verse. A concordance is ideally suited to this kind of Scripture sleuthing.

A word of caution, though: Don't fall prey to the temptation of using a concordance for "proof-texting"—poring over Scripture to find some passage to support your preconceived notions. Danker nettles the conscience when he says:

> ...For someone on the lookout for a particularly appropriate proof text, a concordance is indispensable. As an example, 1 Tim. 2:11 is very handy if the subject of woman's suffrage in the congregation is broached. But to limit the concordance to this function is to sacrifice its magnificent interpretive possibilities.[10]

Proof-texting ignores the fact that God gave us the whole Bible as His revealed Word. It assumes that any nugget of Scripture contains the whole truth, in and of itself. But a mature Bible student knows that every nugget of Scripture truth must be compared with the entire vein of the "mother lode." Sound doctrine cannot be built on a single passage of Scripture, because other passages may clarify or modify the sense of that passage. With this caution in mind, let us consider how to use a concordance most efficiently when we search for a particular verse.

You will probably save time if you look for the most unusual word in any portion of a verse that you recall. The concordance's list of passages for an unusual word should be shorter than the rest. Let's go back to the example at the start of this chapter. Assume you want to find the Bible verse that says, "...He is faithful and just to forgive us our sins and to cleanse us from all unrighteousness."

---

[10]Danker, 11.

If you have an exhaustive concordance, you can find the verse under any word in this quotation. But if you turn to the word *He*, you will find several thousand references. The word *is* has even more references. Trying to find the verse under either of these headings is an overwhelming task.

What about the word *forgive?* Strong's concordance lists 53 occurrences of *forgive* in the KJV. If you happen to know that the verse occurs in the New Testament, you can reduce that number to 25. That's more manageable. If your memory is good enough to recall that the word *unrighteousness* also occurs in the verse, the search gets even easier. (Strong lists 21 occurrences in the entire Bible, 17 in the New Testament.)

Be sure to check other forms of the key word, if you do not find the Scripture passage under the most basic form of the word. For example, Strong's concordance has separate entries for *forgive, forgiven, forgiveness, forgivenesses, forgiveth,* and *forgiving*.[11] So if your memory is a bit hazy about the exact form of this word in the passage you're trying to find, you may need to check the alternate forms of the word. (For verbs, check different tenses. For nouns, check different numbers and genders of the word.)

Of course, this sort of Scripture search is no substitute for memorizing important portions of the Word. We become painfully aware of this when we try to find a verse that has only commonly used words, such as, "In the beginning was the Word, and the Word was with God, and the Word was God." This verse is vital to our knowledge of the eternal nature of Christ. Yet if we try to locate it with a concordance, we find that nearly every word occurs hundreds of times in Scripture. The least common word in this verse is *beginning*; and Strong's concordance lists 106 occurrences of *beginning*. Better to memorize the verse and the reference (John 1:1)!

If you recall a portion of a verse with only very common words, you may be able to use an analytical concordance and look for a key phrase that came from a single Hebrew or Greek word. Let's say you wanted to locate the verse from the Christmas story that

---

[11]Young's concordance gives separate entries for various Hebrew and Greek forms of this word, rather than the various forms of the English rendering.

says, "And they made known abroad the saying which was told them concerning this child."

All of the words are commonly found in the Bible, so focus your search on a phrase such as the verb phrase, "made known." You suppose this English translation comes either from the Greek word for *make* or from the Greek word for *known.* If you go to Strong's concordance, you'll find nearly four full pages of references to *make* and its related verb forms. But if you go to *Young's Analytical Concordance,* you find boldface headings that break up the list according to different Hebrew and Greek words, as well as the different phrases that are derived from these words:

MAKE (ruler), to—
MAKE as though, to—
MAKE away, utterly to—
MAKE (baldness), to—
etc.

Immediately, you see that the phrase, "make known," is not here. So you turn in Young's concordance to the word *known,* where you find these analytical headings:

KNOWN—
KNOWN, to be—
KNOWN, to be fully—
KNOWN, to be made—
KNOWN, to make (to be)—
KNOWN abroad, to make—
etc.

Under that last heading you find this single reference:

To make known throughout, thoroughly,
        Luke 2:17 they made known abroad the saying which

So you find the verse you're after. Unfortunately, Young's concordance does not always help you locate a key phrase. (For example, it does not have a section for "BEGINNING, in the—" to help you with John 1:1). But its analytical format can help you find many of the verses that have common words, by tracing a phrase back to its Hebrew or Greek origin. You also might try *Nelson's Concordance of Bible Phrases* or similar tools.

Suppose you do not recall any portion of the verse itself, but you can recall the subject of the verse. Begin looking under Bible words that may refer to that subject. For example, you may be looking for a verse that deals with God's forgiveness, but you don't recall the exact wording of the verse. One approach is to make a list of Bible words related to God's forgiveness:

> forgive, forgiveness, *etc.*
> grace, gracious, *etc.*
> love, loving kindness, *etc.*
> mercy, merciful, *etc.*

Then you begin checking the passages listed under these words until you come across 1 John 1:9. (This sort of Scripture search is agonizingly slow. If you can remember only the topic of the verse, you may get faster results with a topical Bible, rather than taking this circuitous route with a concordance.)

Two Other Uses: Word Study and Topic Study

How else might you use a concordance, besides locating a Scripture reference that you do not fully recall? Here are some ideas.

Word Study

Explore the richness of a Hebrew or Greek word by using a concordance to find various occurrences of the word in Scripture. Strong's concordance and Young's concordance will help you do this in the KJV.[12] (Unfortunately, the concordances for newer versions seldom furnish the linguistic apparatus you need for this type of study.) Let's see how you can use either of these books to conduct a study of the word *holy* in the Old Testament.

A. *Young's Analytical Concordance.* Turn to the standard English entry, "holy." Beneath it you will find numbered italic subheadings; each one indicates a different Hebrew or Greek term. Here are the first three subheadings under "holy" and "holy, to be—":

1. *Kind,* חָסִיד *chasid.*
2. *Separate, set apart,* קָדוֹשׁ *qadosh.*
3. *Separate, set apart,* קַדִּישׁ *qaddish.*

---

[12]Cruden's concordance does not show the Hebrew or Greek source of a word.

In each case, Young first gives you the literal meaning of the term, then the actual Hebrew or Greek script of the term, and finally the English *transliteration** of that term.

Suppose you decide to study the Hebrew word *qadosh*, the second of Young's subheadings for "holy." You look under *qadosh* and find a list of 56 verses from the KJV, in which the Hebrew word *qadosh* was translated as *holy*. So you select a few of these verses for further study. You then learn that *qadosh* could mean to "separate" a nation from all other nations (Exod. 19:6) or to "separate" oneself from other gods to serve the one true God (Lev. 20:7). The same word refers to a place "separated" from all others, a designated place where God is regularly worshiped (Ps. 65:4) or where religious rituals are performed (Lev. 6:27). Water reserved for Jewish cleansing rituals was "holy," because it was separated from the people's normal bathing water (Num. 5:17). The camp of the Israelites was "holy," in the sense that it was separated from all indecent things (Deut. 23:14). The Sabbath day was "holy," because Sabbath activities for the worship of God were separate from the everyday activities of the community (Isa. 58: 13). All of these insights come from a careful reading of the passages that you find under *qadosh* in Young's concordance.

B. *Strong's Exhaustive Concordance.* Here you must do a bit more work to identify the Hebrew words, but the task is not difficult. Notice the code number printed at the righthand side of each Scripture reference in this sample from the entry "holy" in Strong's:

Ex. 3:5 whereon thou standest is *h·* ground.	6944
12:16 there shall be an *h·* convocation,	"
16 shall be an *h·* convocation to you;	"
15:13 thy strength unto thy *h·* habitation.	"
16:23 of the *h·* sabbath unto the Lord:	"
19:6 of priests, and an *h·* nation.	6918
20:8 the sabbath day, to keep it *h·*.	6942
22:31 and ye shall be *h·* men unto me	6944

These numbers refer to the Bible-language dictionaries that Professor Strong placed at the end of his concordance. A number printed in regular Roman type (as these are) refers to his "Hebrew and Chaldee Dictionary."[13] So you turn to the "Hebrew and Chaldee Dictionary" to find the Hebrew word designated by the code number 6918, as follows:

> 6918, קָדוֹשׁ qâdôwsh, *kaw-doshé*; or
>
> קָדֹשׁ qâdôsh, *kaw-doshé* from 6942; *sacred*
>
> (ceremonially or morally); (as noun)
>
> *God* (by eminence), an *angel*, a *saint*, a *sanctuary*;—
> holy (One), saint.

Strong first gives you the Hebrew script (with a variant script below it), then the English transliteration, followed by a vocalized spelling (how to pronounce the word). He indicates that this word comes "from 6942"—i.e., it is derived from the Hebrew word that Strong assigned the code number of 6942 (*qadash*). Strong gives the literal meaning of the word, "sacred." Following the semicolon, he gives several examples of persons or things that Scripture says are *qadosh*.

Return to Strong's concordance entry *holy* and run your finger down the righthand side of the column. Each time you encounter the number 6918, you have found a verse that uses *qadosh*. Every time you see the number 6942, you have found a verse that uses *qadash*, the root word of *qadosh*. Knowing this, you can proceed with your study and find insights similar to the ones you would find with Young's concordance.

Remember that your purpose in any word study is to grasp and apply the meaning of God's Word. Piling up linguistic data has little value for Christian living, but applying the truth of these biblical words may transform your life.

Topical Study

A concordance can help you review quickly and easily what Scripture says on a certain topic, such as divorce. How is divorce treated in Old Testament, compared to the New Testament? Did God progressively reveal more of His will concerning divorce as human history proceeded? A concordance can give you some insight into this.

---

[13]A code number printed in italic type refers to Strong's "Greek Dictionary of the New Testament."

Alexander Cruden shows his real genius on a topic such as this. He gives us not only a definition of divorce, but a brief commentary on the subject. Notice how Cruden weaves together the Bible's key references to divorce:

DIVORCE

> *Is the dissolution of marriage, or the separation of husband and wife.* Moses *tolerated* divorces; his words on this subject are in Deut. 24:1, 2, 3, 4. When a man hath taken a wife and married her, and it comes to pass that she find no favour in his eyes, because he hath found some uncleanness in her; then let him write her a bill of divorcement, etc. *Commentators are much divided concerning the sense of these words,* because he hath found some uncleanness, *or, as the Hebrew has it,* matter of nakedness, in her.
>
> *The school of* Shammah, *who lived a little before our Saviour, taught that a man could not lawfully be divorced from his wife, unless he had found her guilty of some action which was really infamous, and contrary to the rules of virtue. But the school of* Hillel, *who was Shammah's disciple, taught, on the contrary, that the least reasons were sufficient to authorize a man to put away his wife; for example, if she did not dress his meat well, or if he found any woman whom he liked better. He translated Moses' text thus:* If he hath found any thing in her, or an uncleanness....[14]

Cruden continues with several more paragraphs of explanation. This sort of treatment is seldom found in a topical Bible or other concordance. It makes Cruden's concordance a fascinating volume, though it is a more antiquated one. You will discover Cruden's reliance on folklore about natural history and other subjects by reading his discussion of topics such as *serpent, tongue, unicorn,* or *world.*

Young's and Strong's concordances give linguistic insight into Bible topics rather than theological or cultural commentary. For

---

[14]Alexander Cruden, ed., *A Complete Concordance to the Holy Scriptures* (Old Tappan, NJ: Fleming H. Revell, n.d.), 137.

example, here is what Young's concordance says about divorce and closely related words.

DIVORCE

   A cutting off, כְּרִיתֻת *kerithuth.*

     Jer. 3.8 put her away, and given...a bill of divorce

DIVORCED, to be—

   To loose off or away, 'ἀπολύω *apoluō.*

     Matt. 5:32 whosoever shall marry her that is divorced

DIVORCED, woman—

   To cast out, divorce, גָּרַשׁ *garash.*

     Lev. 21.14 a divorced woman; or profane, (or) an har-
       lot

         22.13 priest's daughter be a widow, or divorced

     Num. 30.9 of a widow, and of her that is divorced

DIVORCEMENT, (writing of)—

   1. *A cutting off* כְּרִיתֻת *kerithuth.*

     Deut. 24.1 let him write her a bill of divorcement

         24.3 and write her a bill of divorcement, and

     Isa. 50.1 the bill of your mother's divorcement

   2. *A setting or standing off or away,* ἀποστάσιον. *apostasion*

     Matt. 5.31 let him give her a writing of divorcement

         19.7 command to give a writing of divorce

     Mark 10.4 suffered to write a bill of divorcement

Notice the various actions that divorce implied to the Hebrew or Greek mind—cutting off, setting loose, casting out, sending away. While the Hebrews considered a divorced woman to be "cast out," the Greeks considered her to be "set loose" or "sent away," given freedom from the marriage bond. What a contrasting image! Reflect upon Young's linguistic notes and you will discern even more about the topic of divorce.

Also notice any developments of the Bible's teaching about a certain topic as you follow the concordance list from the Old Testament to the New. For example, scan this list of selected references from the entry *Passover* in *Nelson's Complete Concordance of the Revised Standard Version Bible,* and watch for changes in Passover practice as history progresses.[15]

it in haste. It is the LORD's p.	Ex 12.11
families, and kill the p. lamb	12.21
is the sacrifice of the Lord's p.,	12.27
...	
"Keep the p. to the LORD your God,	2 Ki 23.21
For no such p. had been kept since	23.22
Josiah this p. was kept to the	23.23
...	
the returned exiles kept the p.	Ez 6.19
they killed the p. lamb for all	6.20
celebrate the feast of the p.,	Eze 45.21
after two days the P. is coming,	Mt 26.02
us prepare for you to eat the p.?"	26.17
I will keep the p. at your house	26.18
...	
release one man for you at the P.	Jn. 18.39
the day of Preparation for the P.	19.14

Several things become evident from this quick reading of the concordance list on *Passover.* (1) The Passover ordinance was established at the time of the Jews' Exodus from Egypt. It commemorated the Lord's "passing over" the Jews, withholding the plague of death from them. (2) King Josiah revived the Passover observance. (3) The Jews revived the Passover again when they returned from the Babylonian Captivity. (4) Jews in New Testament times still celebrated the Passover. (5) Certain customs grew up surrounding the Passover—e.g., the Roman governor's release of a prisoner as a goodwill gesture.

Use care and discernment as you explore a word with the use of a concordance. You will uncover some fascinating insights that you might miss by using a topical Bible for your quest.

---

[15]John W. Ellison, ed., *Nelson's Complete Concordance of the Revised Standard Version Bible* (Nashville: Thomas Nelson, 1957), 1437-8.

ANNOTATED BIBLIOGRAPHY

Several classic Bible concordances were compiled so long ago that their copyright protection has expired. Such books are now in "public domain"—they belong to the public, and anyone may reprint them. So some concordances on this list are available from many publishers. In these cases, I have given the information for one current publisher and indicated with a footnote that other publishers also produce that book.

Cruden, Alexander, ed. *Cruden's Unabridged Concordance.* Ada, MI: Baker Books, 1979.[16]

Early in this chapter, we noted the significant place of Cruden's work in the history of Bible concordances. Some pastors still feel that Cruden's concordance is best, yet Cruden's work is not as complete as Strong's or Young's concordances. It omits some significant passages where a word appears and it does not include proper names. But Cruden's definitions of biblical words make interesting study. (See *church* and *salvation* as examples). Baker's edition contains a sketch of Cruden's life and his "Compendium of the Holy Bible," which summarizes each chapter of Scripture; some publishers omit these features. The chief advantages of Cruden's concordance are its smaller size and lower price, compared to Strong's and Young's. Like them, it is based on the KJV.

Goodrick, Edward W., and John R. Kohlenberger III, eds. *The NIV Exhaustive Concordance.* Grand Rapids: Zondervan, 1990.[17]

This computer-generated concordance contains all key words of the NIV, listing about 250,000 Scripture passages. The editors eliminate most adverbs, prepositions, articles, and other words that occur so often that they are of little help in locating a specific passage. They also insert helpful cross references to take the reader to related verb forms.

---

[16]Also available from (Grand Rapids: Zondervan, 1967), (Cleveland: World Publishing, n.d.), (Uhrichsville, OH: Barbour Publishing, 1993), & (Lebanon, TN: Dugan Publishers, 1986). Abridged editions are available as *Cruden's Compact Concordance* from (Grand Rapids: Zondervan, 1968), and *Cruden's Handy Concordance* from (Grand Rapids: Zondervan, 1988) and (Ada, MI: Baker Books, 1979). A condensed version, *Cruden's Condensed Concordance*, is available from (Lebanon, TN: Dugan Publishers, 1990).

[17]Also available as *The NIV Compact Concordance* (Grand Rapids: Zondervan, 1993) and *The NIV Handy Concordance* (Grand Rapids: Zondervan, 1988).

Morrison, Clinton, ed. *An Analytical Concordance to the Revised Standard Version of the New Testament.* Louisville: Westminster John Knox Press, 1979.[18]

This concordance follows the general pattern of *Young's Analytical Concordance,* but it offers some excellent features not found in Young's. Where the RSV has rendered a Greek word rather freely, Morrison lists the verse with the warning that it is rendered "idiomatically." He follows that with a more literal rendering in brackets. When the RSV supplies a word not in the Greek, Morrison lists the passage under that heading, but he notes that it is used "contextually." His index-lexicon at the back of the book lists various ways a Greek word is translated in the RSV. While this concordance covers only the New Testament, it can be of real help to anyone using the RSV.

Nelson's Concordance of Bible Phrases. Nashville: Thomas Nelson, 1992.

Unlike the traditional Bible concordance that lists tens of thousands of key words, this concordance lists 5,200 memorable phrases from the Bible. This approach dramatically reduces the size of the concordance and makes the search quicker and easier, in most cases. For example, suppose you wish to find the Scripture passage that says, "…You shall know the truth, and the truth shall make you free" Using a complete or exhaustive concordance, you would have to sift through scores of references to common words like *truth, know,* or *free.* But in this concordance, you can turn to the heading, "know the truth," and find that the phrase occurs five times, one of which is John 8:32, the text you're seeking. This concordance is based on the NKJV with cross references to the KJV, NASB, and NRSV.

Strong, James, ed. *Strong's Exhaustive Concordance.* Nashville: Abingdon Press, 1979.[19]

This is by far the most popular concordance based on the KJV because it is the most complete. Dr. Strong accounts for every

---

[18]Several analytical concordances of the NRSV are being prepared as *Swords & Whetstones* goes to press.

[19]*Strong's Exhaustive Concordance* is available in many editions from a variety of publishers. A smaller edition is available as *Strong's Concise Concordance* (Nashville: Thomas Nelson, 1985) and (Chattanooga, TN: AMG Publishers, 1985).

word in the KJV, including insignificant words such as *a, and, it, of,* or *that.* He gives a portion of the verse containing each significant word. (For the very common words such as the ones just mentioned, he provides a list of references without actually quoting the passages.) In an appendix, he includes "A Comparative Concordance of the Authorized and Revised Versions," showing every instance in which the RV or the ASV renders a word differently than the KJV does.[20] He also includes a "Hebrew and Chaldee Dictionary" and a "Greek Dictionary of the New Testament," listing all the Hebrew and Greek words translated by the KJV, with their pronunciation and definitions. This enables you to do Greek and Hebrew word studies, even if you have no prior knowledge of those languages. Some publishers omit portions or all of this appendix from their editions of Strong's concordance. Thomas Nelson has released a compact edition of Strong's concordance under the title, *Strong's Concise Concordance.*

Young, Robert. *Young's Analytical Concordance to the Bible.* Nashville: Thomas Nelson, 1994.[21]

This is the latest edition of Young's classic work, though earlier editions are still being published in Great Britain and North America. Young's concordance is based on the KJV. It has two advantages over Strong's concordance: (1) It gives a brief definition of every word and a description of every person or place, and (2) it identifies each Hebrew or Greek word in the concordance itself, rather than listing them in separate lists with code numbers. These features makes Young's easier to use for Greek and Hebrew word studies. However, Young's also has two distinct disadvantages, compared to Strong's: (1) It does not have references to any word that the KJV translators supplied (the italicized words in the KJV). (2) It often gives key phrases rather than key words, which requires a different approach to word studies, as I explained in this chapter. Despite these disadvantages, many Christian readers prefer to use Young's concordance.

---

[20]Although the ASV and RV are no longer in print, they were forerunners of our current English versions. So Young's "Comparative Concordance" still helps us understand how hundreds of archaic KJV words are translated today.

[21]Also available from (Peabody, MA: Hendrickson Publishers, 1984) and (Cleveland: World Publishing, n.d.).

Chapter 6

Bible Commentaries

The scribe Ezra stood on a wooden platform that had been made for the purpose; and beside him stood Mattithia, Shema, Anaiah, Uriah, Hilkiah, and Maaseiah on his right hand; and Pedaiah, Mishael, Malchijah, Hashum, Hashbaddanah, Zechariah, and Meshullam on his left hand.... Also...the Levites, helped the people to understand the law, while the people remained in their places. So they read from the book, from the law of God, with interpretation. They gave the sense, so that the people understood the reading (Neh. 8:4, 7-8, NRSV).

This seems to be the first record of a popular Bible commentary—"popular" because it was intended to teach the common people, who knew little about their precious heritage of Scripture. They had just returned to Jerusalem after many hard years of captivity in Babylon (586-458 B.C.). During that time, they had begun to adopt the Aramaic language of their captors. Now they could scarcely understand what the Hebrew Old Testament said, much less apply it to their current life. They needed help understanding it, so Ezra's scribes (Heb., *soferim**) "gave the sense" of the Word to the people. As one modern Jewish writer observed, "In their endeavour to cause the people to understand the reading, Ezra and his associates (the *soferim*) had to build bridges between the past and the present...."[1]

"To build bridges between the past and the present" is a good way to describe the task of any Bible commentator! The commentator rephrases the Word in terms that contemporary hearers can understand. He explains how the Word addresses current

---

[1]From I. Epstein's foreword to H. Freedman and Maurice Simon, eds., *Midrash Rabbah*, vol. 1 (London: Soncino, 1939), x. For the brief history of Jewish commentaries that follows, I am also indebted to Hermann L. Strack, *Introduction to the Talmud and Midrash* (New York: Harper, 1965) and to Judah Goldin, trans., *The Living Talmud* (New York: Mentor, 1957).

problems and questions. And the commentator applies the Word to people's needs, discussing the implications of Scripture for their lives today.

Ezra's helpers did that at the Water Gate. The best modern expository preachers continue to do that from their pulpits. Occasionally, a person with this expository gift records that commentary in writing, so that all of us can benefit. These expository studies, written Bible commentaries, are the focus of this chapter.

Jewish Commentaries

To understand better how we came to have the Bible commentaries of today, let's review the history of Jewish Scripture commentaries. The Jewish commentaries set the pattern of Scripture exposition that the early church fathers followed. The rabbis' comments are still quoted in our modern Christian commentaries. In a real sense, then, the Jewish commentaries were the direct ancestors of the Christian Bible commentaries we now have.

The Jews called Ezra and his expositors the "scribes" (*soferim*), because they made new handwritten copies of the ancient Hebrew Scriptures. Since many of the Jews returning from Babylon now spoke Aramaic, the *soferim* began translating the Scriptures into Aramaic as they copied them. These Aramaic translations, called *targums*,* became the common "Bible" of the post-exilic Jews.[2] The scroll that Jesus read in Nazareth probably was an Aramaic targum (Luke 4:10 ff.).

The process of copying and translating the Old Testament into Aramaic was not enough, however. The Jewish worshipers still needed to know how Scripture related to their everyday lives. What could they learn from Scripture that would help them in dealing with their families, their foreign oppressors, and spiritual struggles within themselves?

To answer such questions, the *soferim* began to interpret the Scriptures at public readings. They "gave the sense" of the Scriptures, as Ezra's assistants had done at the Water Gate. Thus, they gave their people an "exposition" (Heb., *midrash* *) of the Law. They explained the meaning of ancient Hebrew names that the

---

[2]J.I. Packer, Merrill C. Tenney, and William White, Jr., eds., *The Bible Almanac* (Nashville: Thomas Nelson, 1980), 345.

Jews no longer used. Occasionally, they made "enactments" (civil-law rulings) to apply the Law of Scripture to contemporary problems. They stated "preventive measures" to insure that a person did not violate the Law. They advised the people of "legal expedients," loopholes in the Law that would permit them to conduct necessary religious activities within the limits set by their captors, without violating the Law.[3]

However, the scribes did not put their commentary in writing. According to Professor Judah Goldin, "Such teaching and legislating as the *soferim* conducted through their schools and councils were carried on orally, in order to carefully distinguish between what was the Written Torah, Scripture, and the body of *exegesis.*"[4]

After about 270 B.C., a few *soferim* who were especially gifted teachers began to mentally organize and memorize these scattered comments. Customarily, these later scribes would repeat a passage of Scripture, interjecting the comments (*midrash*) that various scribes had made about it. These "sages" or "teachers" (Heb., *tannaim*) began each recitation by responding to a question that someone had brought to them. They quoted various Scriptures, the previous scribes' comments (*midrash*) on those Scriptures, and even Jewish legends or folklore that seemed to have some bearing on the subject. This later method of oral recitation and interpretation eventually was called "paragraphing" or "study" (Heb., *mishna*).

We can scarcely comprehend the stupendous feat of memorization that the *tannaim* achieved. Try to imagine a college lecture hall where the students use no notebooks and the lecturer has no written outlines on the chalkboard. Instead of opening a textbook to read the passage under consideration, the lecturer recites each Scripture passage from memory. He interrupts his recitation now and then to make comments on the passage or to answer his students' questions. When he teaches the course the following term,

---

[3]Judah Goldin notes an interesting "legal expedient" recorded in the Mishna: The sages allowed Jews who lived in adjacent houses surrounding a courtyard to prepare food before the Sabbath and leave it at one of the homes. Then on the Sabbath day, they could cross the courtyard to carry food into their homes, even though the Law otherwise forbade them from carrying burdens on the Sabbath. So the "expedients" were also an important kind of commentary on the Law.

[4]Goldin, 23.

he flawlessly recites the passage and its commentary again. He then recites some of the students' questions and his replies from the previous semester! This seems incredible, yet it was the routine method of teaching in the Jewish academies at the time of Christ.

The *tannaim* continued this mental preservation of Scripture commentary for almost five hundred years. During this time, they recognized two major components to their work:

(1) the Law itself and legal rulings based on it (collectively called *halakah* * in Hebrew), and

(2) the legends, traditions, and folklore interwoven with the legal discussions (collectively called *haggadah* * in Hebrew).

Some teachers felt it would not be blasphemous to reduce the *haggadah* to writing, because these teachings did not have the force of divine law. So written collections of *haggadah* commentary were being circulated by about A.D. 200.

By then, the Romans had captured Jerusalem and the Jews had been scattered to the far corners of the Roman Empire. Rabbinical schools had sprung up in Babylon and northern Africa to rival the prestigious academies in Palestine. Judah ha-Nasi and his students in Palestine orally "published" a standard *Mishna* commentary about A.D. 200, but the lecturers at the other academies also began making their own compilations of the *mishna*.

Each academy's collection of *mishna* commentary and its instructors' comments on the *mishna* became known as the "instruction" (Heb., *talmud*). The academies of Palestine compiled their standard *talmud* about A.D. 400; the academies of Babylon formed their *talmud* about A.D. 500. Professor Goldin writes:

> Among other things, the reason the Babylonian Talmud overshadowed the Palestinian—so that in a sense it became *the* Talmud—was that in the centuries after the compilation of the Talmud, the heads of the Babylonian academies pressed hard for its adoption by various Jewish communities; and the political triumph and expansion of Islam put the Babylonian scholars at an advantage. Bagdad [sic] became a most dynamic center, attracting to its academies students from everywhere; in

turn wherever they settled they brought and taught the Babylonian Talmud.[5]

So while marauding Muslim horsemen struck terror in the citizens of Roman Catholic Europe, they also spread Jewish learning by carrying the Babylonian Talmud throughout the Mediterranean world. Abraham Geiger, Isaac Epstein, and other scholars contend that when Mohammed himself wrote the Koran, he based his teachings about the Old Testament patriarchs on this Jewish commentary.[6]

Church fathers including Eusebius, Chrysostom, and Augustine extracted helpful comments on Scripture from the Midrash and Talmud. Nicholas de Lyra, a noted Christian commentator of the fourteenth century and one of Luther's favorite sources, drew many of his ideas from the Midrash. Even today, Christian commentators proudly refer to the biblical insights they have gained from *Judaica* (a Latin term now used to designate Jewish literature in general).

Early Christian Commentaries

In many ways, the growth of Christian commentary on the Scriptures paralleled the growth of Jewish commentary. Church historian Jean Danielou believes the apostolic church at Jerusalem had several converted Jewish scribes in its community, who continued to make *targums* of the Old Testament "but gave it a Christian orientation."[7] The church fathers frequently commented on Old Testament Scriptures; but, unlike the Jewish rabbis, they were quite willing to commit their thoughts to paper. They knew their letters could circulate among all the churches, reaching far more of their Christian disciples than they could ever instruct face to face. So we find a considerable amount of Scripture commentary appearing in these *patristic letters** while the church was still in her infancy.

Clement of Alexandria (ca. A.D. 200) began a major trend in Christian commentaries. He adopted the exegetical ideas of Philo

---

[5]Goldin, 26.

[6]I. Epstein, *Midrash Rabbah*, xx.

[7]Jean Danielou and Henri Marrou, *The First Six Hundred Years*, trans. Vincent Cronin (New York: McGraw-Hill, 1964), 10.

(a Jewish scholar with a large following in that city), who interpreted Bible events as *allegories*.* Philo and Clement believed
Bible history was recorded to illustrate spiritual or moral truth of
enduring value. They believed the events really happened, but
they also felt the Bible preserved these stories to convey deeper
spiritual truths. They felt it was their duty as commentators to
unveil the hidden meaning behind each story.

> At times, [the Apostle] Paul interpreted Old Testament
> events in an allegorical way, as Hellenistic Jewish writ-
> ers often did. The best example is his interpretation of
> the story of Sarah and Hagar. He explained that their
> experience was an allegory of people who still lived
> under the old covenant while others lived under the
> new covenant of Christ (Gal. 4:21-23)
> ...Hellenistic thinkers at Alexandria later developed this
> method of interpretation to its height.[8]

Philo and the other Jewish scholars of Alexandria used allegory to interpret the Jewish Scriptures; now Clement and his Christian colleagues continued the trend. Danilou notes that "Clement
used the method with discretion; in his writings the various
sources are easy to disentangle. If he borrows from Philo an allegory about Sara and Abimelech, he first gives Philo's interpretation, then works out another, more christological...."[9]

Clement's successors at the Christian academy of Alexandria
were not so cautious, however. Radical allegory colored the work
of Philo's star pupil Origen, as well as the commentaries of Justin,
Irenaeus, Melito, Tertullian, and other men rooted in the Alexan-
drian tradition. Some used numerology, mysticism, and classical
mythology to interpret Scripture. A good example is Hippolytus'
Commentary on Daniel (A.D. 203). Danker says, "They often oblit-
erated the original intent of the [biblical] writers with a maze of
fanciful exegesis both astounding and depressing to behold."[10]

A different commentary tradition began with Diodorus, Bishop
of Tarsus. Before becoming bishop in A.D. 376, Diodorus served as

---

[8]Packer *et al.*, *The Bible Almanac*, 174.
[9]Danilou and Marrou, *Six Hundred Years*, 129.
[10]Frederick W. Danker, *Multipurpose Tools for Bible Study*, 2nd ed. (St. Louis:
Concordia, 1966), 254.

a priest in Antioch, where another Christian academy was being formed to rival the one in Alexandria. To all intents, Diodorus functioned as head of that school. He was an outspoken *apologist** and an excellent writer. He urged his students to interpret all of Scripture, both Old and New Testaments, in the most literal way possible. He cautioned them to avoid looking for hidden spiritual meanings or taking every major Bible event as a symbol or "type" of something in the future.

Diodorus' literal method of Bible interpretation influenced the work of Jerome, Augustine, and other prestigious Christian writers; but these men still preferred the allegorical method. The literal approach became the predominant method of Christian commentary only after the Reformation.

While the Babylonian Talmud was being circulated in the Jewish world, the two major Christian academies (at Alexandria and at Antioch) developed their own distinctly different methods of doing biblical commentary. Through *encyclical letters,** apologetic treatises, and actual books of Bible commentary, the scholars in these two schools of Bible commentary "gave the sense" of the Old Testament to their Christian friends. They applied New Testament teachings to the theological and ethical problems faced by the church as it spread into strange cultures and encountered new challenges.

Medieval and Reformation Commentaries

During the Middle Ages, Christian scholars made great strides in commentary work. Theophylact, the Metropolitan of Bulgaria, wrote a series of brilliant commentaries on the New Testament and most of the Old during the eleventh century. Bede the Venerable and Anselm also were writing practical commentaries at this time.

Then the sixteenth-century Reformation loosed a flood of Christian biblical commentaries. Unlike commentators before them, the Reformers stressed a literal interpretation of Scripture. Martin Luther (1483-1546) and John Calvin (1509-64) wrote profound, penetrating commentaries that challenged lay readers to renew their interest in the literal meaning of God's Word. Luther wrote only on selected books of the New Testament, while Calvin completed a 45-volume set on the entire Bible. Soon came more Protestant commentaries by Matthew Poole (1624-79), Matthew Henry (1662-1714), John Gill (1697-1771), and a host of others.

The seventeenth and eighteenth centuries became an age of ponderous, rambling commentaries. When a Bible student comes across one of these venerable sets in a bookshop today, he wonders how any reader had enough patience to plow through the thousands of pages of exposition (usually in very small print). Perhaps it is a tribute to our ancestors' appetite for God's Word.

The nineteenth and twentieth centuries brought a continuation of the classical modes of commentary, but added an emphasis on exposition based on pastoral ministry. Charles H. Spurgeon, Dwight L. Moody, Alexander MacLaren, Arthur W. Pink, Donald Barnhouse, and other well-known Christian commentators of this period were pastors or evangelists, rather than academicians. Their work largely consists of transcripts from their expository sermons. This gives their commentaries a focus on the practical application of Scripture in everyday life.

What to Expect

Pastors and Sunday school teachers hold a wide range of opinions on the value of Bible commentaries. Many laymen complain that commentaries are too difficult to use, too expensive, and not likely to provide new insights about a given passage. Spurgeon heard similar complaints. He wrote:

> It has been the fashion of late years to speak against the use of commentaries.... Usually, we have found the despisers of commentaries to be men who have no sort of acquaintance with them; in their case, it is the opposite of familiarity which has bred contempt.[11]

As Spurgeon suggests, the lingering discontent with commentaries may not be so much the fault of the commentaries themselves as it is of the readers, who expect too much. If we believe that a commentary will make plain everything that is obscure in Scripture or resolve every doctrinal argument that may arise—we are sure to be disappointed! We need to have a realistic idea of

---

[11]Charles H. Spurgeon, *Commenting and Commentaries* (Carlisle, PA: Banner of Truth. 1969), 1.

what a good Bible commentary should do.

First, a commentary should present the message of Scripture as clearly as possible. Some commentators become so preoccupied with their own pet interests (linguistics, archaeology, sociocultural backgrounds, systematic theology, or whatever) that they fail to give a clear reading of the Word. Yet that is essential. The commentary may provide a fresh translation of the Scriptures, along with the commentary. This can help the reader's understanding, as long as the commentator does not distort the translation to suit other purposes.

Second, a commentary should explain any confusing words or phrases. Check a few selected passages to see whether the commentator does this. For example, does he attempt to explain what the phrase "other tongues" means in Acts 2:4? Or, "They are not all Israel, which are of Israel" (Rom. 9:6)? Or, "the order of Melchisedek" (Heb. 6:20)? The commentator may not be able to give a fully satisfying explanation of these terms, but he should offer some enlightenment.

Third, a commentary should identify the major themes of the biblical book. Many of the commentator's remarks must deal with specific words or phrases in the text; but if the commentary leaves you with only that, you may not comprehend the actual message of the Scripture text. The commentator should point out the main thrust of the Bible writer's message, so you can see how various parts of the passage contribute to the overall message. Look for an outline, an introductory essay, or both, discussing the major themes of the Bible book.

Fourth, a commentary should sketch the cultural background against which the book was written. The commentator should set the stage on which the events of the biblical narrative are enacted. The writer should review any events that prompted the writing of the book. He should describe the readers for whom the book was originally intended. All of these factors will enlarge your grasp of what you read.

Types of Commentaries

Various commentaries are described as "devotional," "exegetical," "expository," and so on. You should know the differences between them, since types of commentary are suited to specific methods of study.

A *devotional* commentary is designed to give some inspiring thoughts on the Scriptures, without much detailed analysis of the text or involved theological reasoning. Most of today's devotional commentaries come from sermons by well-known pastors or radio evangelists.

A *practical* commentary is a specific type of devotional commentary that emphasizes the application of Scripture to daily living. The commentator may do this by asking a series of questions that probe your present spiritual condition. He may give examples of other Christians who faced problems and found answers from Scripture. Or he may use other methods to challenge you to put God's Word into practice.

A *scholarly* commentary uses extensive research to unlock the subtle meanings of each Scripture passage. The Christian scholars of medieval times prided themselves on reading everything they could find on a given subject, and compiling all the pertinent information in their essays. The modern scholarly commentator is likely to take a similar approach. He quotes what other commentators have said about the text, about a particular word, or about the person or event under study. Then he draws his own conclusions, trying to show why his view is the most reasonable.

An *expository* commentary is the most common type of scholarly commentary. This term comes from the Latin word *expositio*, which means "explanation." The expository commentator explains the message of the text by using relevant insights from linguistics, theology, and ancient history. Often he will cite a variety of other writers who have commented on this passage, and he will outline the logical unfolding of the biblical writer's message.

An *exegetical* commentary is the most sophisticated type of scholarly commentary. This term comes from the Greek word *exēgeesthai*, which means "to lead out." The exegetical commentator "leads out" or "draws out" the meaning of each phrase or word in the original Hebrew and Greek texts. He will include a greater number of word studies along the way and may also cite recent archaeological finds from ancient scrolls or papyrus fragments that provide a better understanding of certain words. Of course, you will find various degrees of exegesis in various commentaries. Some are fairly easy for a layperson with no technical knowledge of the Hebrew and Greek, while others require a foundational knowledge of these ancient languages.

How to Use Commentaries

Bible students are tempted to expect Bible commentaries to do all interpretation of the Bible for them. Pastors are tempted even more, because they feel pressured to produce a continuous stream of good Bible lessons for others, so they often have several commentaries within reach. It's easy for a pastor to pull three or four commentaries from the shelf, compare what they say about a given passage, and knead these comments into an outline to suit his purposes. Sunday school teachers might do the same.

But Bible commentaries should not be used as substitutes for personal Bible study. They are aids to your own deliberate, prayerful thinking. With that end in mind, here is a step-by-step method for using Bible commentaries, which will work with any type of Bible study. (See the various Bible study methods reviewed in Chapter 1.)

1. *Pray that God will help you understand what you read.* The psalmist prayed, "Make me to understand the way of Your precepts; so shall I meditate on Your wonderful works" (Ps. 119:27). The apostle Paul told his friends in Ephesus, "Therefore I also…do not cease not to give thanks for you, making mention of you in my prayers; that the God of our Lord Jesus Christ, the Father of glory, may give to you the spirit of wisdom and revelation in the knowledge of Him, the eyes of your understanding being enlightened…" (Eph. 1:15-18a).

God reveals Himself through the Bible. He expects you to see Him there and He expects you to understand what you see. So it is appropriate to pray that He will help you understand Scripture. You can be sure that as you pray, He will give you "the spirit of wisdom and revelation" for studying His Word.

2. *Read and reread the Bible passage you plan to study.* You may miss the full impact of the passage the first time through, so review it. In fact, you may want to speed-read it the second time to get the thematic "drift" of the passage. Ask yourself, What is the core of this Scripture passage? What is its basic message?

3. Read the Bible passage in another version for comparison. Chapter 2 explained how to compare versions of different kinds. You may find that an unfamiliar version sheds a different light on the passage you are studying. It may seem to give the passage an altogether different meaning! (If that's the case, refer to a good exegetical commentary to see which Bible version is giving you the most accurate rendering of the Hebrew or Greek.)

4. Outline the Scripture passage. On a piece of paper, note the key thought of the passage. Notice how the passage develops that thought, step by step. This is especially helpful when you read poetic passages such as those in Proverbs or Psalms, or complex theological passages like those in Romans or Galatians. Your own study outline will enable you to see the skeleton of the passage. It shows how seemingly unrelated statements can supplement the theme of the Bible text.

5. Reflect on what this Bible passage means for your life. As long as you leave the Bible's teaching in the abstract, theoretical realm, you will get little benefit from it. But when you begin applying a Scripture passage to your life, God will use the Bible study to transform you. (Consider 1 John 4:11-14 or Jude 14-16, for example.)

Notice that you still haven't consulted a Bible commentary to this point. You have relied on what God's Holy Spirit reveals as you ponder the Scripture text and what your own reasoning may discover in the passage. Only then should you...

6. Consult a commentary for further insights. Instead of letting the commentary provide the substance of your study, let it shape your study after you have begun. A good commentary will provide facts about Bible culture or history that you may not be able to gather through personal study and reflection on the text. It will point out subtle nuances in the Hebrew or Greek, which the English versions might not convey. It will correct any tendency toward *heterodox** or *heretical** doctrine based on one passage, by referring you to other Bible passages that more fully explain God's truth about the issue.

I believe that if you follow this six-step pattern, you will gain the minimum benefit from a Bible commentary. The commentary will become a help instead of a hindrance to your study. It will be a walking stick instead of a crutch.

Watch that "Slant"!

Thirty years ago, I was a newspaper reporter. In newspaper writing, we carefully had to avoid giving a biased "slant" to our articles. A reporter can bias a reader's opinion by omitting some of the facts, making snide remarks, or describing the subject in derogatory terms. The reporter may not even realize that such a bias has crept into the article. (That's one reason why we have editors!)

Bible commentaries may be slanted, too. Like a biased reporter, a Bible commentator may omit certain facts. He may ignore or detract from other points of view because he feels his interpretation of a certain passage is the only true interpretation. He may slant the comments to his own way of thinking, perhaps without realizing it.

Of course, you should expect a commentator to share his opinions with you, especially when you come to obscure passages of Scripture. But the commentator does a disservice if he omits contradictory facts or views in hopes of strengthening his argument. You do yourself a disservice if you consult only commentaries that are slanted to suit our own views. When Charles H. Spurgeon drew up a catalogue of Bible commentaries for ministerial students, he warned that he was including many books with which he disagreed. He said:

> Where we have admitted [to the catalogue] comments by writers of doubtful doctrine, because of their superior scholarship and the correctness of their criticisms, we have given hints which will be enough for the wise. It is sometimes very useful to know what our opponents have to say.[12]

That's good advice for any reader of commentaries! Proceed with caution. Watch for the slants. (See Figure 15.) Yet appreciate the rich diversity of views among the commentators.

When buying a commentary for a friend, you may need to be even more cautious, because you do not want to buy one with a slant that will offend. I believe it is seldom wise to buy a Bible version or Bible reference book as a gift, unless you know specif-

---

[12]Spurgeon, 34.

ically what your friend wants or needs. (When in doubt, give your friend a bookstore gift certificate.)

Higher Criticism

Besides doctrinal bias, a commentator's approach to higher criticism can also affect the content of the commentary. Chapter 2 pointed out that textual criticism is often called "lower criticism" because it is the entry level of serious Bible study. Further stages of serious Bible study, where we consider the meaning of Scripture, are called "higher criticism."

Bible commentators disagree about how to do higher-critical study. A commentator may feel so strongly about certain higher-

Figure 15
Scripture Passages That Reveal A Commentary's Theological Bias

---

What a Bible commentator says about the following passages may reveal any theological "slant":

Arminianism*—Deut. 5:10, 29; Ps. 33:13-15; Matt. 10:22; 24:10-13; Acts 10:28; Rom. 9:4ff.; Col. 1:22, 23; Heb. 3:6, 14; 6:11-12.

Calvinism*—Prov. 16:4; Jer. 1:4-5; John 6:37-44; Rom. 4:4-5; 9:4ff.; 11:5-6; 1 Cor. 15:10; 2 Thess. 2:13; 1 Pet. 1:3-5.

Unitarianism*—Deut. 6:4; 1 Kings 8:60; John 1:1; 17:3; 1 Tim. 2:5; Phil. 2:5-11.

Universalism*—Isa. 29:18-24; 52:13-15; 57:15-21; Matt. 18:1-4, 10-14; Luke 3:5-6; 1 Tim. 4:10.

Dispensationalism—Rom. 2:28-3:31; Eph. 1:10-11; 2:11-19; 3:2-6; Col. 1:24-27; Heb. 1:1-2; 8:8-12.

Amillennialism*—Matt. 25:31-46; Mark 13:32-37; Acts 1:6-7; 1 Cor. 15:51-52; 1 Pet. 3:3-10; Rev. 20.

Premillennialism*—Isa. 65:19-25; Zech. 9:9-10; 14:16-17; Heb. 8:11; Rev. 20.

Postmillennialism*—Luke 18:7-8; 1 Cor. 15:24-28; Col. 3:1-4; Eph. 1:10; Rev. 20.

Rapture and Tribulation—Matt. 24:21-31, 40-44; Luke 21:35-36; 1 Thess. 4:15-17; 2 Thess.2:3.

critical methods that he uses the commentary to promote them. Be aware of the methods of higher criticism that a Bible commentator may employ, because distortions of the Bible's meaning may be caused by inappropriately using some of these. Here are the most common higher-critical methods:

Form criticism*—The German scholar Hermann Gunkel (1862-1932) developed this method. He observed that nearly every generation has its unique style of oral or written history-keeping. This unique style ("form") may identify which generation created a piece of literature. Thus, if the history of a certain event began as an oral record and was later put into writing, the written account would still bear some marks of the oral version. Gunkel believed he could identify several "forms" in the Old Testament—i.e., several layers of oral tradition. So he analyzed sections of Scripture to try to determine when certain portions of them originated and who originated them. Martin Dibelius, Rudolf Bultmann, and other scholars have used form criticism to analyze the New Testament as well.

Literary criticism (or "source criticism")—For centuries, Christian scholars have examined the literary style and the cultural background of various books of the Bible. Origen (second century A.D.) compared the style of the Epistle to the Hebrews with the known epistles of Paul, then declared that Paul had not written Hebrews. His student Dionysius compared the Gospel of John and the Book of Revelation, concluding that John had not written both of those books, because the two styles were so different.

Today's literary critics try to use the literary styles of Scripture to ascertain the authorship, date, and place where each book of the Bible was written. For example, some feel that the Book of Genesis was written and/or edited by scribes from four different eras of Israel's history. (This idea is known as the "documentary hypothesis."[13]) Others believe that two, three, or more individuals wrote the Book of Isaiah.

---

[13]A recent popular treatment of the documentary theory is Richard Elliott Friedman's *The Hidden Book of the Bible* (San Francisco: Harper San Francisco, 1998). It contains Friedman's own compilation of the narrative supposedly written by "J," an anonymous author from the southern kingdom of Judah who referred to God as YHWH ("Jehovah").

Obviously, a literary critic can employ a variety of methods to arrive at these conclusions. To a great extent, he must rely on his own opinions to interpret what he finds.

Redaction criticism*—Gerhard von Rad (1901-71) and other Old Testament scholars pointed out that the writer of Deuteronomy was actually making a revised edition of the earlier Mosaic law of Exodus, restating some of the laws to conform with a later theological view. Martin Dibelius noticed a similar pattern in the Gospels of Matthew and Luke. He believed they had reworked the history of Mark to suit their own purposes. Such a study of how a biblical writer may have edited older written material is called redaction criticism, from the German word *redakteur* ("editor").

Commentators use these methods and a host of others, such as "audience criticism" and "canon criticism," to explore basic questions about a passage of Scripture: Who wrote it? When? Why? To whom? After a commentator has considered what the writer meant in the original setting where the Scripture passage took shape, he moves on to consider what the passage means for us today.

There are fundamental differences in the way that liberal and conservative commentary writers use higher criticism. Generally speaking, the liberal commentator believes that the Bible is a collection of writings by individuals with a variety of theological views. He uses higher criticism to sort out these strands of thought and to judge which strands provide greater theological understanding. W.F. Albright, Raymond E. Brown, and Martin Dibelius are some of the best-known writers who take this approach.

The conservative commentator believes that the Bible is basically the work of one Author, the Holy Spirit, who worked through a variety of human authors to produce the Scriptures. So conservatives use higher-critical methods to show the unity of the Bible. F.F. Bruce, C.F. Keil, and Edward J. Young are some writers who have done this.

ANNOTATED BIBLIOGRAPHY

Hundreds of Bible commentaries are now available and the titles chosen for this bibliography are written from a variety of theological perspectives. We have tried to avoid books that show a

marked bias or distortion of the meaning of Scripture. We have listed only works that are currently in print, though some excellent
commentaries are out of print. Also, while this book focuses on
Christian resources, you also should consult some of the excellent
Jewish commentaries on Scripture. You will find the latest publication data in the current edition of *Books in Print* (New York:
R.R. Bowker, annual).

WHOLE BIBLE

Albright, W.F., and David Noel Freedman, general editors, *The
Anchor Bible*, 59 vols. projected. Garden City, NY: Doubleday,
1964- .

This ecumenical commentary includes volumes by Jewish,
Roman Catholic, and Protestant scholars. Conservative readers
dislike the liberal higher-critical approach in several volumes,
such as the lengthy discussion of the documentary theory in E.A.
Speiser's volume on Genesis. However, *The Anchor Bible* gives
excellent background information about the Bible languages and
recent archaeological findings that shed light on Scripture. Raymond E. Brown's two volumes on the Gospel of John and Markus
Barth's on Ephesians are perhaps the best to date. Each volume of
The Anchor Bible contains the commentator's own translation of
the book being considered.

Black, Matthew, and H.H. Rowley, eds. *Peake's Commentary on
the Bible*. New York: Routledge, 1997.

This is one of the best conservative commentaries based on
the New Revised Standard Version. (The other is *The New Bible
Commentary*.) Peake's delves into some rather thorny theological
problems, so laymen may fear that it is "over their heads," but this
volume yields rich rewards to anyone who does concentrated
study. This edition contains a helpful series of Bible maps.

Brown, Raymond E., Joseph A. Fitzmeyer, and Roland E. Murphy,
eds. *The Jerome Biblical Commentary*. Paramus, NJ.: Prentice-Hall,
1986.

Named in honor of the brilliant fourth-century scholar who
penned the Latin Vulgate, *The Jerome Bible Commentary* is an

outstanding Roman Catholic work. Barber points out that this commentary "supplies a remarkable contemporary interpretation which at times is at variance with accepted Catholic doctrine" (ML, 46). Despite these variances, *The Jerome Bible Commentary* will be a standard for Roman Catholic readers for many years to come. Most of the writers are American.

Buttrick, George A., ed. *The Interpreter's Bible*, 12 vols. Nashville: Abingdon Press, 1958.

On each page, this commentary offers parallel texts from the King James Version and the Revised Standard Version, with commentary alongside. This gives the reader a good way to compare versions that use quite different manuscripts as their source. The KJV and RSV tend to balance one another textually. The chief disadvantage of this arrangement is that it leaves little space for the actual commentary. *The Interpreter's One-Volume Commentary on the Bible* (Nashville: Abingdon Press, 1971) contains only the commentary. A new edition of *The Interpreter's Bible* is being released in the near future.

Calvin, John. *Calvin's Commentaries*, 22 vols. Ada, MI: Baker Books, 1974.

Though not as well known as his *Institutes of the Christian Religion*, these commentaries also exhibit Calvin's keen insight into spiritual and ethical matters. Spurgeon observes that "of all commentators I believe John Calvin to be the most candid. In his expositions he is not always what moderns would call Calvinistic; that is to say, where Scripture maintains the doctrine of predestination and grace he flinches in no degree, but inasmuch as some Scriptures bear the impress of human free action and responsibility, he does not shun to expound their meaning in all fairness and integrity. He was no trimmer and pruner of texts" (CC, 4).

Earle, Ralph, editor. *Adam Clarke's Commentary on the Bible.* Cleveland: World Publishing, 1996.

This classic Wesleyan-Arminian commentary was first published in London in 1844 as six volumes. Clarke's languid, meandering style in that original set was more appropriate to the days of long reading hours, but is a bit exasperating today. Dr. Ralph

Earle, former professor at the Nazarene Theological Seminary, has deftly cut out Clarke's less relevant comments to produce this meaty volume.

Gaebelein, Frank E., ed. *The Expositor's Bible Commentary*, 12 vols. Grand Rapids: Zondervan, 1976-92.

This commentary on the NIV utilizes much of the research that the translators did as they worked on the NIV itself. It provides good word studies and a conservative evangelical view of authorship and dates. It is a thorough and scholarly work, offering helpful linguistic insights.

Motyer, J. Alec. and Gordon J. Wenham. *The New Bible Commentary: Revised*, 3rd ed. Downers Grove, IL: InterVarsity, 1994.[14]

Here's a good example of European evangelical Bible commentary, though it is a bit uneven in depth. Its treatment of the Gospels or the New Testament *General Epistles*,* for example, is more meticulous than its treatment of the *Major Prophets*.* Even so, it does deal with most of the difficult words and phrases in each passage. The commentary's supplemental articles are also helpful. Most of the writers of *The New Bible Commentary* come from a Reformed Church background. This commentary is based on the NRSV.

Harper, A.F. and W.T. Purkiser, eds. *The Beacon Bible Commentary Series*, 10 vols. Kansas City, MO.: Beacon Hill Press, 1964-69.

This Wesleyan-Arminian commentary often quotes earlier commentators' views on a given passage instead of offering any new insights. It occasionally dips into critical studies of the Hebrew or Greek, but would have been strengthened by more detailed word studies. While the introductions are quite brief, they do give the overall theme of each book and an outline. The commentary has detailed discussions of messianic prophecies and most Pauline Epistles, with shallow treatment of biblical covenants and eschatology.

---

[14]A Spanish edition of this commentary is available under the title *Nuevo Comentario Biblio*, trans. Tito Eafasuli et. al. (El Paso, TX: Casa Bautista de Publicaciones, 1986).

Harrison, Everett F., and Charles F. Pfeiffer, eds. *Wycliffe Bible Commentary*. Chicago: Moody Press, n.d.

Forty-eight evangelical American scholars contributed to this work, which is highly regarded by conservative evangelical Christians. Its chief weakness is that it does not treat many passages in depth, but the exposition of the text is sound so far as it goes.

Henry, Matthew. *A Commentary of the Whole Bible,* 6 vols. Old Tappan, NJ: Fleming H. Revell, 1980.[15]

Henry's work is undoubtedly the favorite devotional commentary among Protestant readers. He deals with the KJV as it is, exploring the practical implications of Scripture for daily living. Henry employs quaint illustrations from his own age (he was a pastor in Chester, England in the late 1600s), and some of these illustrations are now difficult to understand. Yet his wisdom and spiritual maturity are clearly evident. Spurgeon told his students, "Every minister ought to read Matthew Henry entirely and carefully through once at least. I should recommend you to get through it in the next twelve months after you leave college" (CC, 3).

Howley, G.C.D., F.F. Bruce, and H.L. Ellison, eds. *The New Layman's Bible Commentary*, 24 vols. Nashville: Broadman & Holman Publishers, 1978-94.

This British-based commentary project has a *neo-orthodox** slant. The writers reject Moses' authorship of the Pentateuch and the unity of the Book of Isaiah. The scholarship is good and the comments are easy to grasp, although most conservative readers will reject its conclusions.

Hubbard, David A., and Glenn W. Barker, eds. *The Word Biblical Commentary*. 52 vols. projected. Waco: Word, 1982- .

This series promises to be the first major exegetical commentary produced by conservative American scholars in our generation. The volumes issued thus far have been thorough and original.

---

[15]Also available in six volumes from (Grand Rapids: Zondervan, 1961) and as one volume editions from (Grand Rapids: Zondervan, 1981); (Waynesboro, GA: OM Literature, 1995); (Peabody, MA: Hendrickson Publishers, 1991); (Nashville: Thomas Nelson, 1997); and for the NIV from (Grand Rapids: Zondervan, 1992).

Each writer makes his own new translation of the text. A section called "Comment" gives an exegetical treatment of key Hebrew or Greek words, while another section called "Explanation" expounds the practical meaning of the passage. This series could rival the *New International Commentary* sets.

Jamieson, Robert, A.P. Fausset, and David Brown. *Jamieson–Fausset–Brown Bible Commentary*, 3 vols. Peabody, MA: Hendrickson Publishers, 1997.[16]

First published in 1871, this was one of the earliest English-language commentaries to grapple with the Hebrew and Greek linguistics of the Bible. Most of the early textual insights of Jamieson, Fausset, and Brown have been supported by subsequent discoveries such as Egyptian papyri and the Dead Sea Scrolls. It remains a basic resource for any serious Bible student.

Maclaren, Alexander. *Expositions of Holy Scripture*. 17 Vols. Ada, MI: Baker Books, 1977.

This is actually a series of expository sermons in which Maclaren led his congregation through the Bible. The series does not focus on key words or phrases in Scripture; rather, it deals with the major themes, devoting a chapter (i.e., a sermon) to each theme. *Maclaren's Expositions* make enjoyable devotional reading and some professors recommend that ministerial students read the series to learn expository preaching.

McGee, J. Vernon. *Thru the Bible*. 5 vols. Nashville: Thomas Nelson, 1995.

A modern counterpart to *Maclaren's Expositions*, this commentary is superior to it in many respects. McGee does devote some attention to key Hebrew and Greek words, explaining them in terms that laymen may readily understand. He also answers many of the questions raised by modern cults and heterodox Bible teachers. At the core, *Thru the Bible* is a pastoral work. It shows Dr. McGee's deep concern for applying God's Word to everyday situ-

---

[16]Also available in one volume as *Jamieson, Fausset and Brown's Commentary on the Whole Bible* from (Grand Rapids: Zondervan, 1979).

ations, a skill that he learned during his pastorates in Nashville, Dallas, and Los Angeles. Dr. McGee was a conservative evangelical.

Ogilvie, Lloyd J. *The Communicator's Commentary*, 12 vols. projected. Waco: Word, 1982- .

This is the first complete commentary based on the NKJV. It attempts to build a bridge between the scholarly commentaries, which are too technical for lay readers, and the devotional commentaries, which often fail to investigate the full implications of the text. Writers in this series include Earl Palmer, Myron Augsburger, and other well-known expository preachers.

OLD TESTAMENT

Gibson, John C. L. *The Daily Study Bible: Old Testament*, 24 vols. Louisville: Westminster John Knox Press, 1987.

This series is intended to be a companion to William Barclay's New Testament commentaries by the same name, though it takes a noticeably more liberal theological stance than Barclay's work. Gibson endorses the documentary hypothesis (the idea that several different editors compiled the Pentateuch). Unlike Barclay, he minimizes the *typological** significance of the Old Testament. He also finds immediate fulfillment to many prophecies that most conservative readers would consider to be end-time prophecies. Despite his departure from Barclay's track, Gibson gives us a good scholarly commentary in the liberal tradition.

Hubbard, Robert L. Jr. *The New International Commentary on the Old Testament*, 22 vols. Grand Rapids: William B. Eerdmans Publishing Company, 1976-98.

Already winning a reputation as the most thorough Old Testament commentary produced by evangelical American scholars, the NICOT provides meaningful Hebrew word studies and sets the cultural backdrop of Old Testament events. Laymen may feel that the NICOT is too technical to suit their purposes. However, the challenging content of the series is well worth concentrated study.

Keil, C.F., and Franz Delitzsch. *Keil & Delitzsch Commentary on the Old Testament*, 10 vols. Peabody, MA: Hendrickson Publishers, 1996.

Because they engage in word studies even more than the NICOT, Keil and Delitzsch's work is foreign to many lay readers. But ministers recognize it as the standard Old Testament commentary written from a conservative viewpoint. The original work was published more than fifty years ago. Osborne and Woodward observe that Keil and Delitzsch's commentary is "still unsurpassed for general exegetical excellence" (HBS, 121).

Wiseman, Donald J., ed. *Tyndale Old Testament Commentaries*, 26 vols. Downers Grove, IL: InterVarsity, 1981-96.

Compact and inexpensive, the Tyndale series has become a layman's favorite. Most of the contributors are British evangelicals. When the first volumes appeared, one bookseller stated that the Tyndale series would be popular because the "comments are very helpful, yet not so lengthy as to tire the reader" (*Christianity Today*, Feb. 5, 1982, 99).

THE PENTATEUCH

Mackintosh, Charles Henry. *Genesis to Deuteronomy*. New York: Loizeaux Brothers, 1972.

As a devotional commentary, Mackintosh's work ranks alongside Matthew Henry's for its simplicity and human interest. American evangelist Dwight L. Moody praised this as a good commentary for new Christians to read. The volume reflects Mackintosh's dispensationalism and other Plymouth Brethren doctrines.

Genesis

Pink, Arthur W. *Gleanings in Genesis*. Chicago: Moody Press, 1966.

Pink likes to interpret Scripture in terms of allegories and "types," and perhaps he tries too hard to find them. He attempts to draw symbolic lessons from all the objects or events of biblical history. Despite these occasional excesses, Pink does breathe life into many Genesis passages that we might otherwise take for granted.

Exodus

Davis, John J. *Moses and the Gods of Egypt*. Winona Lake, IN: BMH Books, 1985.

Recently discovered papyrus documents in Egypt describe the elaborate religious system of the pharaohs. Davis uses this information to reexamine Moses' confrontation with the hardhearted Pharaoh Amenhotep II. This makes a lively and interesting study.

Pink, Arthur W. *Gleanings in Exodus*. Chicago: Moody Press, 1964.

Pink's commentary on Exodus is a good devotional study. His search for types and allegories is as persistent as it was in his Genesis commentary. That does not obscure the spiritual insight he brings to most passages, however.

Leviticus

Kellogg, Samuel H. *Studies in Leviticus*. Grand Rapids: Kregel Publications, 1988.

This commentary also deals with the symbolism of the Levites' ceremonies, but not in as much detail as we find in Pink's commentary. Kellogg gives more emphasis to the historical impact that Jewish civil laws had upon their worship. This book was originally part of the classic *Expositor's Bible* series.

Numbers

Jensen, Irving L. *Numbers: Journey to God's Rest-Land*. Chicago: Moody Press, 1968.

Jensen is a respected teacher of inductive Bible study methods and his expertise is obvious here. He shows how to penetrate Numbers' bewildering mass of laws and statutes to find their meaning for God's relationship with man. The reader can learn much about the inductive method of Bible study by following Dr. Jensen through this study.

Deuteronomy

Schultz, Samuel J. *Everyman's Bible Commentary: Deuteronomy.* Chicago: Moody Press, 1971.[17]

Professor Schultz of Wheaton College has given us this brief but well-informed commentary. It reveals his knowledge of modern archaeological research and his sound exegetical method.

THE HISTORICAL BOOKS

Crockett, William D. *A Harmony of Samuel, Kings, and Chronicles.* Ada, MI: Baker Books, 1985.

This classic work, first published in 1897, offers a consecutive history of Israel's and Judah's kings from the parallel accounts of the Old Testament. Crockett dispels many apparent contradictions in these accounts.

Thiele, Edwin R. *The Mysterious Numbers.* Grand Rapids: Kregel Publications, 1994.

Here Thiele unravels the dates of the kings' coronations and deaths by showing that the historians of Israel and Judah used two different dating systems. This fascinating study contradicts most earlier attempts to fix the dates of these events. It also supports the "early date" of the Exodus, which conservative scholars insist was about 1440 B.C.

Joshua

Hamlin, E. John. *Inheriting the Land: A Commentary on the Book of Joshua.* Grand Rapids: William B. Eerdmans Publishing Company, 1983.

A conservative expository treatment of Joshua, this volume explains many customs of the Jewish priestly tradition. Hamlin draws on the latest archaeological and linguistic insights to create a commentary that truly breaks fresh ground in the study of this important Old Testament book. Yet his writing style is direct and simple.

---

[17]Also available as *Deuteronomy: El Evangelio del Amor* (Grand Rapids: Kregel Publications, 1979).

Redpath, Alan. *Victorious Christian Living.* Old Tappan, NJ: Fleming H. Revell, 1993.

Redpath's devotional study complements the more serious exegesis of Davis' commentary cited above. It does not examine Joshua in a systematic fashion, but it does point out practical lessons God's people may learn from the book. Redpath borrows heavily from Alexander Maclaren's devotional comments.

Judges-Ruth

McGee, J. Vernon. *Ruth: The Romance of Redemption.* Nashville: Thomas Nelson, 1997.

This reprinting is welcome because Dr. McGee brings to light several aspects of Ruth's personality that would escape the notice of a casual reader. He shows colorfully how Ruth's story illustrates God's redemption of mankind.

Ezra-Nehemiah-Esther

Ironside, H.A. *Joshua, Ezra, Nehemiah, Esther.* New York: Loizeaux Brothers, 1983.

Ironside does not plow very deeply into the cultural or historical material of these books, but he does draw many practical lessons from them. This early dispensationalist preacher had a tendency to look for allegories and types in unlikely places.

Job

Barnes, Albert. *Notes on the Old Testament, Explanatory and Practical: Job.* Ada, MI: Baker Books, 1983.

Barnes' *Notes* have been well known for many years, and this is one of the best commentaries in the series. Spurgeon said, "The student should purchase this work at once, as it is absolutely necessary to his library" (CC, 75). Barnes capably deals with the issues of theodicy* as raised by the Book of Job.

Psalms

Spurgeon, Charles H. *The Treasury of David,* 7 vols. Grand Rapids: Kregel Publications, 1977.[18]

This book reveals the expository genius of Charles H. Spurgeon, long-time Baptist pastor of the Metropolitan Tabernacle in

---

[18]Also available in 3 volumes, edited by David O. Fuller (Peabody, MA: Hendrickson Publishers, 1988).

London. Spurgeon had a gift for discerning the practical application of Scripture; he had an equally remarkable gift for eloquent
speaking and writing. Both gifts make *The Treasury of David* a
treasure indeed. The American pastor Wilbur M. Smith wrote,
"This is one set of books no minister will ever sell, unless he has
lost faith in the Word of God, and no longer intends to preach or
teach" (PBS, 145).

Proverbs

Bridges, Charles. *The Geneva Commentary Series: Proverbs.* Carlisle,
PA: Banner of Truth, 1979.

Reviewers agree that Bridges' commentary is "the classic" work
on Proverbs (BLBS, 15; CC, 104; ML, 106). Perhaps his greatest
strength is his skill at relating the Proverbs to other parts of Scripture. Bridges shows how the practical, ethical truth of this book
resurfaces again and again throughout the written Word.

Song of Solomon

Bernard of Clairvaux. *Bernard of Clairvaux: On the Song of Songs*,
trans. Kilian Walsh and Irene M. Edmonds, 4 vols. Kalamazoo, MI:
Cistercian Publications, Inc., 1971-81.

The medieval Abbot of Clairvaux has given us the most extensive commentary on the Song of Solomon as a spiritual allegory.
Bernard's sermons interpret the symbolism of this book from
every conceivable angle. This is a fascinating devotional study.

Falk, Marcia. *Love Lyrics from the Bible.* Livonia, MI: Almond Press.
1982.[19]

Falk concludes that the Song of Solomon is not a spiritual allegory; neither does she believe it is a ballad of King Solomon's
courtship. "In its earliest stages, the Song was probably not a uni-
fied work at all," she observes, "but several lyric poems each having its own integrity" (p. 3). Falk's masterful study gives the
Hebrew text (which the author has divided into 31 lyric poems),
a poetic translation, and six essays on the work. This is the first

---

[19]Also available as *The Song of Songs* (San Francisco: Harper San Francisco,
1990) and *The Song of Songs: A New Translation and Interpretation* (San Francisco: Harper San Francisco, 1993).

original study of this Old Testament book in many years. Though it is a novel interpretation, all Bible students should consider it.

Ironside, H. A. *Proverbs, Song of Solomon*. New York: Loizeaux Brothers, 1933.[20]
Ironside believes this love poem is a double allegory—first of God's love for His chosen people, then of Christ's love for His church. He draws many lessons about Christ's self-sacrifice for the church, the church's submission to Christ, and related themes. Ironside writes from a dispensationalist perspective.

THE MAJOR PROPHETS

Isaiah

Young, Edward J. *The Book of Isaiah*, 3 vols. Grand Rapids: William B. Eerdmans Publishing Company, 1992.
Dr. Young advocates the traditional view that Isaiah wrote this entire prophecy. He describes Isaiah's messianic prophecies with reverence and interprets the end-time predictions with an amillennial approach. Young's three-volume set seems to be the best conservative commentary on Isaiah published thus far. Young comes from a Reformed Church background.

Jeremiah-Lamentations

Jensen, Irving L. *Everyman's Bible Commentary: Jeremiah*. Chicago: Moody Press, 1966.[21]
Very simply written, this inductive study is well-suited to the beginning Bible student. It also makes a good discussion springboard for group study.

Laetsch, Theodore F.K. *Jeremiah-Lamentations*. St. Louis: Concordia, 1996.
This Lutheran writer discusses God's wrathful judgment of Judah in a way that helps us realize His pending judgment of modern society. Laetsch points out the grievous injustices in Judah that led to the nation's fall. As he does, we can see clear similari-

---

[20]Also available as part of *The Ironside Commentaries Series* (New York: Loizeaux Brothers, 1996).
[21]Also available in Spanish from (Grand Rapids: Kregel Publications, 1996).

ties to the injustices in modern Western society.

Daniel

Walvoord, John F. *Daniel: The Key to Prophetic Revelation*. Chicago: Moody Press, 1970.

Dr. Walvoord, long-time president of Dallas Theological Seminary, interprets the Book of Daniel with a premillennial viewpoint. He cites many recent archaeological finds that aid our understanding of the Babylonian climate in which Daniel was writing. This evidence helps to confirm that Daniel wrote the book.

THE MINOR PROPHETS*

Boice, James Montgomery. *The Minor Prophets*, 2 vols. Grand Rapids: Kregel Publications, 1996.

Dr. Boice was for many years the popular radio speaker for the "Bible Study Hour" and pastor of Tenth Presbyterian Church in Philadelphia. He brings a true expositor's gift to these volumes, which offer perceptive insight into the message of the Minor Prophets without distracting erudite language.

Feinberg, Charles L. *Minor Prophets,* rev. ed. Chicago: Moody Press, 1976.

As a converted Jew, Dr. Feinberg brings a sensitive heart to this discussion of God's judgment on ancient Israel. He emphasizes the need for repentance, not only by the Old Testament Jews, but by every person who tries to be spiritually self-sufficient. This is a revised edition of Dr. Feinberg's five-volume series entitled, *Major Messages of the Minor Prophets*, which originally was published by the American Board of Missions to the Jews. He interprets end-time prophecies with a premillennial perspective.

Hosea

Mays, James L. *The Old Testament Library: Hosea*, ed. G. Ernest Wright, et al. Louisville: Westminster John Knox Press, 1969.

Barber feels this is "one of the better works" in the OTL series (ML, 115). Dr. Mays examines the theory that two different writers composed this book, and he uses literary criticism to discern various strands of authorship in the book. Yet the overall thrust of

Mays' commentary is not on dissecting its authorship, but on explaining the relevance of Hosea's message for today.

Jonah

Martin, Hugh. *The Geneva Commentary Series: Jonah.* Carlisle, PA: Banner of Truth. 1995.

This thorough commentary by a nineteenth-century Scottish Presbyterian leader has plenty of spiritual meat for modern readers. Spurgeon called it "a first-class exposition of Jonah... No one who has it will need any other" (CC, 137).

Micah

Mays, James Luther. *The Old Testament Library: Micah.* Louisville: Westminster John Knox Press, 1976.

Professor Mays of Union Theological Seminary (Richmond, VA) has written a brilliant analysis of Micah. He uses liberal methods of higher criticism, but not in a polemical way. We don't get the impression he has any liberal theological agenda, but a genuine desire to examine the prophet's message.

NEW TESTAMENT

Barclay. William. *The Daily Study Bible*, 18 vols. Louisville: Westminster John Knox Press, 1975-1976.

The compact size of each volume makes this set handy for classroom use or personal travel. Barclay gives his own translation of each passage, followed by his commentary, which is largely devotional. Barclay thinks along neo-orthodox lines, so both liberal and conservative readers can find valuable teaching here.

Bruce, F.F., ed. *The New International Commentary on the New Testament,* 18 vols. projected. Grand Rapids: William B. Eerdmans Publishing Company, 1960- .

The editors at Eerdmans explain that this is a series "serving the interests of both pastor and scholar" (BRW, 27). It is a monumental project. The introductory articles themselves read like major research essays, yet the introductions and commentaries are easy for the educated layman to understand. They explore the richness of the Greek language and generally provide a conservative solution to textual problems. The entire set is excellent.

Hendriksen, William. *New Testament Commentary*. Ada, MI: Baker Books, 1953- .

A conservative writer of great clarity, Dr. Hendriksen provides a simple commentary that holds true to the evangelical tradition. "He always sees the practical side of God's truth," Wiersbe writes (BLBS, 19). Hendrickson favors an amillennial interpretation of prophecy.

Muck, Terry, gen. ed. *The NIV Application Commentary*, 11 vols. Grand Rapids: Zondervan, 1995-98.

The editors of this commentary pursue the goal of applying Scripture to modern life. They emphasize practical ways to live what the Bible teaches, rather than evaluating the relative trustworthiness of ancient manuscripts or debating controversial theories about ancient culture. The author of each volume is an evangelical Protestant. They have used the NIV as the basis text for their work. The result is a commentary that ordinary people can use every day, knowing that it's written by scholars who will honor conservative theological convictions.

Keener, Craig S. *The IVP Bible Background Commentary: New Testament*. Downers Grove, IL: InterVarsity, 1993.

"…This book is not written primarily for scholars, who already have access to much of this information elsewhere. But pastors and other Bible readers who have fewer resources and less time available need a concise and handy reference work in one volume at their disposal" (p. 17). With these words the author sets the tone for the ambitious task of commenting on the entire Bible from a scholarly perspective, for readers who are not specialists in the field. Dr. Keener has done an admirable job on both counts. Having taught at Duke University and Hood Theological Seminary, he engages the reader with the eagerness of a passionate instructor who knows how to draw novices into the complex study of biblical cultures.

Lenski, Richard C.H. *An Interpretation of the New Testament*, 12 vols. Minneapolis: Augsburg Fortress Press, 1933-46.

This is one of the few recent commentaries written from an Arminian and amillennial vantage point. Lenski analyzes the Greek text carefully, but not pedantically. He argues against premillennialism, but in favor of infant baptism and consubstantiation. Some volumes drop out of print at various times, but you should be able to find most of Lenski's commentaries on the epistles of Paul.

Tasker, R.V.G. *The Tyndale New Testament Commentaries*, 20 vols. Grand Rapids: William B. Eerdmans Publishing Company, 1957-71.

This set does not delve as deeply into Greek syntax and idioms as does the *New International Commentary on the Old Testament.* It is also less expensive, since it is bound in paperback. The British writers who predominate the staff of this project show a neo-orthodox slant in their theology.

Wesley, John. *Explanatory Notes upon the New Testament*, 2 vols., Kansas City, MO: Beacon Hill Press, 1981.[22]

Wesleyan readers will delight in this reprint of Wesley's own interpretation of key New Testament passages. He lifts up the doctrines of universal atonement, prevenient grace, sanctification of the believer, and other concepts that most other commentators do not address. It is a valuable supplement to any standard commentary set.

THE GOSPELS

Royster, Archbishop Dmitri. *The Parables: Biblical, Patristic and Liturgical Interpretation.* Crestwood, NY: St. Vladimir's Seminary Press, 1996.

Archbishop Dmitri of the Orthodox Church in America takes the reader on a thoughtful exploration of 27 parables from Jesus' teaching in the Gospels. He enlists the early Church Fathers and traditional liturgical texts to help us apply the parables. This brief book summarizes each story and sets forth a sound interpretation

---

[22]Also available from (Salem, OH: Schmul Publishing Co., 1976) and in 3 volumes (Salem, OH: Schmul Publishing Co., 1975.)

of the text. In keeping with Orthodox tradition, Archbishop Dmitri favors the allegorical interpretation of Scripture. This approach is most appropriate with Jesus' parables, which the Lord presented as allegories.

Scroggie, W. Graham. *A Guide to the Gospels*. Grand Rapids: Kregel Publications, 1995.

Scroggie plumbs the theological depths of the Gospels. His work is well-suited to a serious, thoughtful reader who wishes to know as much as possible about the Person and work of Christ. Barber observes that Scroggie's commentary is "worth an entire shelf of books on the same subject" (ML, 139).

Ylvisaker, Johannes. *The Gospels*. Milwaukee: Northwestern Publishing House, 1977.

This unique commentary has a long history, being first published in Norwegian in 1905, then in English in 1932 and reprinted after long neglect in 1977. Ylvisaker gives us a Gospel synopsis (a gathering of all four Gospels' accounts of a particular event in Jesus' life), followed by commentary. It's a conservative expository study and a good introduction to the Gospels as a whole.

Matthew

Crosby, Michal H. *Spirituality of the Beatitudes: Matthew's Challenge for First World Christians*. Maryknoll, NY: Orbis Books, 1981.

Based upon his years of involvement in efforts to bring social justice to various parts of the world, Crosby's commentary on the Beatitudes challenges the complacency of most Western Christians in the face of human need. Devotional and often anecdotal, *Spirituality of the Beatitudes* challenges all of us to love the needy in a sacrificial way, as Christ does. Crosby is a Roman Catholic author and uses the New American Version as the text for this work.

Montague, George T. *Companion God: A Cross-Cultural Commentary on the Gospel of Matthew*. Mahwah, NJ: Paulist Press, 1989.

Father Montague's colorful commentary on Matthew draws frequently upon his experiences in various Third-World countries to illustrate the text. For example, to show the caste-defying act of

Jesus' healing the leper (Matt. 8:1-4), Father Montague shares the experience of a young seminary student working in a leprosarium of India, where castes and leprosy are still familiar facts of life. The commentary is lucid and practically oriented. The author's consistent use of Third-World experience to illustrate the text will widen many Westerners' understanding of the gospel. Montague includes the RSV text of Matthew in its entirety.

Mark

Swete, H.B. *Kregel Reprint Library: Commentary on Mark*. Grand Rapids: Kregel Publications, 1978.

Evangelical reviewers recommend this more than any other commentary on Mark. Swete has a reputation for clear, perceptive analysis of Scripture, and this volume confirms it. Be sure to consult this classic, even though Swete did not have the benefit of some ancient fragments of Mark that archaeologists have uncovered since his time.

Luke

Godet, Frederic L. *Kregel Reprint Library: Commentary on Luke*, Herndon, VA: Books International, Inc., 1981.

Godet probes the meaning of virtually every phrase in Luke's gospel. His commentary is an invaluable resource for studying any portion of Luke, and you are apt to return to it again and again. Barber says it "deserves a place on the shelf of every pastor" (ML, 147).

John

Pink, Arthur W. *An Exposition on the Gospel of John*, 4 vols.. Grand Rapids: Zondervan, 1968.

For an easy-to-understand devotional commentary on John, Pink's is the best choice. His comments are simple but not superficial, perceptive but not radical. This commentary would be superb for a deductive study of John's Gospel. It surveys the major themes of the book without detailed word studies or cultural comments.

Acts of the Apostles

Jensen, Irving L. *Acts: An Independent Study.* Chicago: Moody Press, 1973.

Dr. Jensen, who long served as professor of Bible at the conservative Bryan College in Dayton, Tennessee, is a leading proponent of inductive Bible study. This study of Acts is his best by far. It is an excellent laboratory for learning the inductive method of Bible study.

Romans

Barnhouse, Donald Grey. *Expositions of Bible Doctrine.* Grand Rapids: William B. Eerdmans Publishing Company, 1966.

This series of expository sermons by a famed Presbyterian pastor will inspire anyone who reads it. While Dr. Barnhouse focuses on the contemporary significance of Romans, he does not lose sight of the gradual development of the church's understanding of this book. The commentary is actually an informal study of historical theology, and a first-rate study at that.

Hodge, Charles. *A Commentary on the Epistle to the Romans*, rev. ed. Grand Rapids: William B. Eerdmans Publishing Company, 1993.

Hodge's thorough commentary is acclaimed as one of the best evangelical studies of Romans. Dr. Hodge was a leader of the evangelical minority at Princeton Seminary in the mid-1800s. His writings are strongly Calvinistic, but even non-Calvinists will value his analytical treatment of Romans.

Käsemann, Ernst. *Commentary on Romans*, trans. Geoffrey W. Bromiley. Grand Rapids: William B. Eerdmans Publishing Company, 1994.

Käsemann is a conservative German scholar, and he handles the Epistle of Romans with respect for its normative influence upon the early church. This commentary is being well-received in America as pastors become better acquainted with it.

Luther, Martin. *Commentary on Romans*, trans J. Theodore Mueller. Grand Rapids: Kregel Publications, 1976.

This commentary was excerpted from the notes that Luther used in his historic series of lectures at Wittenberg University in 1512-13. During this lecture series, God revealed to Luther the full impact of the statement, "The just shall live by faith" (Rom. 1:17). Ironically, Luther has little to say about that specific passage here. He provides a much fuller discussion of justification in his commentary on Galatians, but this commentary on Romans still holds real historical interest.

1 Corinthians

Morris, Leon. *The Tyndale New Testament Commentaries: First Corinthians*, ed. R.V.G. Tasker. Grand Rapids: Eerdmans, 1988.

Reviewers agree that this is one of the best volumes of the TNTC. Morris perceives the basic themes of Paul's letter to the Corinthians, and he describes those themes clearly and simply. Morris' treatment of 1 Corinthians 12–14, concerning spiritual gifts, is especially helpful.

2 Corinthians

Hughes, Philip E. *The New International Commentary on the New Testament: Paul's Second Epistle to the Corinthians*. Grand Rapids: Eerdmans, 1994.

Barber believes this commentary "may well be regarded as the finest conservative exposition of this epistle!" (ML, 166). I would agree, at least as far as modern commentaries are concerned. Hughes applies excellent Greek scholarship to the letter and gives us a thorough analysis of the doctrinal terms Paul uses.

Galatians

Luther, Martin. *Commentary on St. Paul's Epistle to the Galatians*. Ada, MI: Baker Books, 1979.[23]

John Bunyan said, "I prefer this book of Martin Luther's (except the Bible) before all the books I have ever seen, as most fit for a

---

[23]Also available as *Commentary on Galatians* (Grand Rapids: Kregel Publications, 1987) and (Old Tappan, NJ: Fleming H. Revell, 1987) and as *Commentary on Galatians: Modern English Edition* (Old Tappan, NJ: Fleming H. Revell, 1994).

wounded conscience" (CC, 176). Indeed, Luther's commentary on Galatians brings us the full flower of his teaching on justification. The reformer's doctrine of "salvation through faith alone" was firmly rooted in Paul's epistles to the Romans and the Galatians; so this commentary gives us an intimate view of the Bible study that shaped Luther's life work.

Ephesians

Lloyd-Jones, D. Martin. *Exposition of Ephesians*, 8 vols. Ada, MI: Baker Books, 1973-87.

Study these sermons for good models of expository preaching. They reflect the fervor and wisdom of a mature pastor. Both minister and layperson can profit from the insights in these messages which the late Dr. Lloyd-Jones preached at Westminster Chapel in England. The discourses are conservative, well-reasoned, and practical.

Moule, Handley C.G. *Ephesians*, 2nd ed. Fort Washington, PA: Christian Literature Crusade, 1982.

Here is a good devotional commentary that focuses on the nature of the church. Moule's style of writing is a bit more difficult to follow than most devotional works, but his deep theological insights are worth the attention.

Philippians

Lightfoot, J. B. *Crossway Classic Commentaries Series: Philippians*. Wheaton, IL: Crossway Books, 1994.

We should expect an impeccable piece of New Testament Greek scholarship from Lightfoot, an eminent Bible translator of the early twentieth century, and he does not disappoint us. His commentary contains a revised Greek text of the entire epistle, with textual notes in which Lightfoot dissects the meaning of every significant Greek word and phrase. This commentary is too sophisticated for most laymen, but pastors and other advanced students will love it.

Colossians-Philemon

Lightfoot, J.B. *Commentary on the Epistles of St. Paul to the Colossians and Philemon*, 4 vols., rev. ed. Grand Rapids: Zondervan, 1992.

Deep, scholarly analysis of the Greek text is the hallmark of Lightfoot's work. His background articles on the culture of the times and the teachings of various Jewish and Christian sects are also quite good. Lightfoot was one of the leading liberal Bible scholars of this century.

Moule, Handley C.G. *Studies in Colossians and Philemon*. Grand Rapids: Kregel Publications, 1977.

Moule's exegesis of the Greek text is not as thorough as Lightfoot's. His theological tendencies are more conservative as well. Evangelical lay readers will prefer this volume because it is not as academically sophisticated as Lightfoot's.

1 and 2 Thessalonians

Collins, Raymond F. *The Birth of the New Testament: The Origin and Development of the First Christian Generation* (New York: Crossroad, 1993).

Father Collins introduces us to First Thessalonians with a meticulous study of Hellenistic Judaism, showing how clearly the early church departed from the synagogue customs of that day. His serious, scholarly examination of the text provides a thorough series of Greek word studies that reveal the subtle nuances of Paul's message to the Thessalonians. The result is a commentary that college and seminary students can use with profit, yet one that does not lose touch with the everyday concerns of parish ministry. Father Collins unearths some fascinating clues in this, the earliest of Paul's letters.

Martin, D. Michael. *The New American Commentary: 1,2 Thessalonians*. Nashville: Broadman & Holman Publishers, 1995.

The New American Commentary is an *exegetical** series written by leading Southern Baptist scholars of North America, based on the NIV. Martin's volume on Thessalonians is exceptionally thorough in its analysis of how Paul used the Greek language. It is a useful reference book for pastors as well as ministerial students.

THE PASTORAL EPISTLES

Dibelius, Martin, and Hans Conzelmann. *Hermeneia: The Pastoral Epistles*, ed. Helmut Koester. Minneapolis: Augsburg Fortress Press, 1972.

The *Hermeneia* series is produced by leading liberal Bible scholars, mostly from Europe. This volume is one of the best in the series. Dibelius and Conzelmann draw upon the apostolic fathers, Hellenistic philosophers, and rabbinic sources to paint the cultural background of the *Pastoral Epistles**. They give a moderate interpretation of controversial passages (e.g., 1 Tim. 2:12 on women's roles in the church; 1 Tim. 5:17 ff. on the duties of presbyters; and 2 Tim. 3:16 on the purpose of Scripture).

Hendriksen, William and Simon J. Kistemaker. *New Testament Commentary: Exposition of Thessalonians, the Pastorals, and Hebrews.* Ada, MI: Baker Books, 1996.

This excellent study interprets Paul's words about the return of Christ in an amillennial fashion. Hendriksen offers many insights from the early church fathers and from recent archaeological discoveries at Thessalonica, insights not found in older or more devotional commentaries.

Ramsey, William M. *Historical Commentary on the Pastoral Epistles,* ed. by Mark Wilson. Grand Rapids: Kregel Publications, 1996.

Archaeology buffs will recognize the name of Sir William M. Ramsay (1851-1939), one of the eminent pioneers of modern biblical archaeology. Ramsay provides good insight into the culture of New Testament times and the cultural challenges that an emerging church had to overcome. He highlights the fact that Paul devotes considerable attention to Christian family life in these epistles. Sir Ramsey emphasizes that strong, spiritually mature families are vital to a healthy church.

Stott, John R.W. *Guard the Truth: The Message of 1 Timothy and Titus* (Downers Grove, IL: InterVarsity, 1996).

A leading British evangelical, Stott focuses on Paul's theme of the church as the defender of the Christian faith. Stott finds here a wealth of practical counsel for pastors and lay leaders, especially in an age when secular society presses the church to blend the gospel with the teachings of various religions and philosophies. The commentary includes a useful study guide for small-group discussion.

1 and 2 Timothy

Hiebert, D. Edmond. *Everyman's Bible Commentary: I and II Timothy,* 2 vols. Chicago: Moody Press, 1957-58.[24]

Here is a fascinating devotional commentary—a bit more technical than most, but full of inspiring ideas. Young ministers will appreciate these volumes because Hiebert makes Paul's advice to a young pastor relevant for today. Lay leaders will benefit by reading them, too.

THE GENERAL EPISTLES

Martin, R.A., and John H. Elliott. *Augsburg Commentary on the New Testament: First and Second Peter, James, Jude.* Minneapolis: Augsburg Fortress Press, 1982.

A thoughtful expository work, this commentary on the General Epistles draws many parallels between the New Testament epistles and Old Testament literature. However, it is not too technical for the layperson.

Hebrews

Brown, John. *The Geneva Commentary Series: Hebrews.* Carlisle, PA: Banner of Truth, 1983.

Bible students were very happy to see the Banner of Truth reprint this classic of 1862. Brown rambles a great deal, but he covers some real gems of spiritual truth along the way. His discussion of the Hebrew tabernacle is especially good.

---

[24]Also available as *Primera y Segunda Timoteo* (Grand Rapids: Kregel Publications, 1988).

Hughes, Philip Edgcumbe. *Commentary on Hebrews.* Grand Rapids: William B. Eerdmans Publishing Company, 1987.

Wiersbe says this commentary is "essential for your library; I cannot recommend it too much!" (BLBS, 25). Others may not be so enthusiastic, especially if they disagree with Hughes' literal interpretation of Old Testament "types." Even so, this commentary ranks with F.F. Bruce's NICOT volume as one of the best evangelical expositions of Hebrews published in recent years.

MacArthur, John. *Hebrews.* Chicago: Moody Press, 1983.

Well-known evangelical pastor and radio minister John MacArthur gives us a fine pastoral commentary on Hebrews. He emphasizes the epistle's teaching of the preeminence of Christ, couched in Jewish ritual terms that first-century Christians could readily understand. The exposition is clearly and colorfully presented. One could read it for its inspirational value as well as its instructional value. MacArthur's staunch Calvinism, which dominates some of his other books, is scarcely noticeable here.

Murray, Andrew. *The Holiest of All: An Exposition of the Epistle to the Hebrews.* Ada, MI: Revell, 1993.

First published in 1894, Murray's devotional commentary on Hebrews is a classic study in biblical typology. He explains how the Old Testament tabernacle displayed physically how God relates spiritually to His people. Thus, he believes, the tabernacle was a "type" of the redemptive work of Christ. Murray's elaborate Victorian writing style may discourage readers who are accustomed to breezy contemporary books, but they will find significant theological depth here.

Owen, John. *Hebrews: The Epistle of Warning.* Grand Rapids: Kregel Publications, 1973.

The noted Scottish theologian Thomas Chalmers called Owen's commentary "a work of gigantic strength as well as gigantic size" (CC, 188). Owen traces the most minute detail of symbolism from this book back to the Old Testament, and attempts to explain the spiritual significance of it. You will find plenty of good insights here, but you must sift through heaps of speculation to get at them. Kregel's one-volume abridgment helps.

James

Hawkins, O.S. *Getting Down to Brass Tacks: Advice from James for Real World Christians.* (New York: Loizeaux Brothers, 1993).

Pastor of First Baptist Church in Fort Lauderdale, O.S. Hawkins brings a skillful blend of pastoral and exegetical commentary to this book. He concentrates on James' teachings of Christian ethics and morality, yet he does not drift into a simplistic mode of pre-scription. Hawkins guides us from one key Greek theological word to another, showing how James' moral mandates grew out of a deeply-anchored relationship with God.

Palmer, Earl F. *The Book that James Wrote.* Grand Rapids: William B. Eerdmans Publishing Company, 1997.

A noted conservative Presbyterian pastor and author, Dr. Palmer offers this brief (104-page) pastoral commentary on an epistle that is a favorite for small-group study. Unlike most commentaries, which keynote James' ethical teachings, Palmer's work traces the theme of faith in this epistle. What is faith? How does faith grow strong or ebb away? What are the consequences of neglecting our faith? Palmer deals helpfully with these issues in the context of James' letter.

1 and 2 Peter

Marshall, I. Howard and ed. by Grant R. Osborne. *The IVP New Testament Commentary: 1 Peter.* Downers Grove, IL: InterVarsity, 1991.

This volume by a respected British Methodist scholar is one of the best in InterVarsity's New Testament series. While bringing scholarly skill to the task of exposition, Professor Marshall con-tinuously applies the counsel of Peter to modern Christian life. He finds in 1 Peter a reliable guide to how we can live as responsible disciples in a hostile world.

Jowett, John Henry. *The Epistles of Peter.* Grand Rapids: Kregel Pub-lications, 1993.

Kregel has reprinted this classic commentary by English Con-gregationalist J.H. Jowett (1864-1923), whose work is not as well-known today as it was a generation ago. Jowett's pastoral com-mentary tends to be more speculative than those of modern writ-ers. He frequently explores the byways of "what if?" theorizing. Yet he is guided by a conservative, well-tempered conscience that keeps even his speculation to the task of finding Peter's practical relevance to today's reader.

1, 2, and 3 John

Hiebert, D. Edmond. *The Epistles of John: An Expositional Commentary*. Greenville, SC: Bob Jones University, 1991.

Dr. Hiebert sets forth the traditional view that the Apostle John wrote these three epistles as well as the Gospel narrative that bears his name. He also defends the traditional conservative interpretation of the epistles. Yet Hiebert gives opposing views a hearing at every juncture, making this a fair-minded study in the Johannine letters. An awkward feature is the commentary's reliance on the KJV text, which does not reliably render the Greek at many points. Dr. Hiebert is careful to point out any discrepancies between the KJV and the Greek, as well as to offer sensible answers to these dilemmas. (See, for example, his comments on 1 John 3:20.) All in all, he gives us a sound evangelical treatment of the epistles.

Sloyan, Gerard S. *Walking in the Truth: Perseverers and Deserters*. Valley Forge, PA: Trinity Press International, 1995.

Sloyan has produced a handy exegetical commentary which can only discuss selected passages because of its brevity (96 pages). It is a significant book because it offers a current Roman Catholic view of John's letters. Sloyan often cites with approval the interpretations of the late Raymond A. Brown, who was the best-known Catholic scholar of recent years. The commentary endorses liberal theories of the authorship of these epistles. It discusses their message with an even-handed respect for the various interpretations made throughout the years.

Revelation

Newell, William R. *The Book of the Revelation: Chapter by Chapter*. Grand Rapids: Kregel Publications, 1994.

This premillennial interpretation, first published in 1935, is now considered one of the best conservative commentaries on Revelation. Newell propounds the premillennial, pretribulational return of Christ in a well-reasoned but emphatic way. This study is good for beginning students who wish to understand the premillennial view of the End Time.

Strong, Marie, and Sharon Pearson. *A Common-Sense Approach to the Book of Revelation.* Anderson, IN: Warner Press, 1996.

Dr. Strong developed this book while teaching introductory New Testament courses at Anderson University. Dr. Pearson completed the work after Dr. Strong's death. Both women bring to the task a familiarity with the concerns of lay readers. The result is a concise, amillennial commentary on Revelation, which applies the message of this book to a Christian's daily life.

Walvoord, John F. *The Revelation of Jesus Christ.* Chicago: Moody Press, 1966.

Walvoord strongly expounds the premillennial return of Christ. As former president of Dallas Theological Seminary, he was an influential leader in evangelical circles. He articulates the approach that most modern evangelicals take to Revelation—i.e., that it predicts literal events which will occur in history, and that the symbols and "signs" of Revelation can help us ascertain when Christ's return is near.

Chapter 7

Bible Dictionaries, Encyclopedias, and Handbooks

The reference-book section of a Christian bookstore offers you a delightful variety of Bible dictionaries and encyclopedias. Many have full-color photographs of Holy Land sites and up-to-date information on archaeologists' work, which often confirm or clarify the history of the Bible. Some of these reference books are popularly written; others are academic. One researcher has noted that more Bible dictionaries and encyclopedias have appeared in the last 250 years than all other biblical study aids put together.[1] So there is an enticing abundance of Bible knowledge to explore here.

We can use these books to fill the gaps of our Bible knowledge. For example, the Scriptures may mention in passing a city such as Carchemish or Pergamos, with no details about the military or commercial importance of the city. Or the Scriptures may mention a powerful king, general, or other secular leader such as Cyrenius and Tiberius, without explaining his impact upon secular history. Perhaps a religious custom, doctrine, or concept is mentioned in the Bible, with little explanation of how that practice originated. A Bible dictionary or encyclopedia will explain such things as far as Bible scholars can explain them. These books are valuable supplements to a good Bible commentary, which must be concerned with the Scripture text itself.

Suppose you are studying the Book of Hosea. A good Bible commentary will provide background information about the political climate of Hosea's day, the impending collapse of his nation, the impact of Hosea's stern preaching, and so on. The commentary also may note some interesting incidental facts, such as the Hebrew divorce decree (Hos. 2:2) or the price of a slave bride (Hos. 3:2). But if you want to learn more about Jezreel (the ancient city for which Hosea named his first son), you could look

---

[1]Charles T. Fritsch, quoted in *Recommending and Selling Biblical Reference Works* (Grand Rapids: William B. Eerdmans Publishing Company, 1980), 18.

up *Jezreel* in a Bible encyclopedia or dictionary, where you would find information like this:

JEZREEL (jĕz´rē-ĕl, jĕz´rēl, Heb. *yizre'el, God soweth*).

1. A city on the border of the territory of Issachar (Josh. 19:18), not far from Mount Gilboa. The Israelites made their camp near it before the battle of Gilboa (1 Sam. 29:1), its people remaining faithful to the house of Saul. Abner set Ishbosheth over it among other places (2 Sam. 2:9). Ahab built a palace there (1 Kings 21:1), and his son Joram also lived there (2 Kings 8:29). Naboth was a Jezreelite, and he was stoned outside the city for refusing to give up his vineyard to Ahab (1 Kings 21). Jehu ordered that the heads of Ahab's 70 sons be placed in heaps at the gate of Jezreel (2 Kings 10:1-11)....[2]

With this information, you can imagine how Hosea's Jewish friends must have felt when the prophet named his firstborn for that city. Either he had terribly poor taste or God had directed him to choose this name for a peculiar reason. (See Hos. 1:4-5.)

Perhaps you are puzzled by Paul's exhortation in 1 Thessalonians 5:26: "Greet all the brethren with a holy kiss." So you turn to the word, *Kiss,* in a Bible dictionary and find an explanation like this:

Kiss. Kissing the lips by way of affectionate salutation was customary among near relatives of both sexes.... Between individuals of the same sex, and in a limited degree between those of different sexes, the kiss on the cheek as a mark of respect or an act of salutation has at all times been customary in the East, and can hardly be said to be extinct even in Europe. In the Christian Church the kiss of charity was practiced not only as a friendly salutation, but as an act symbolical of love and Christian brotherhood. Rom. 16:16; 1 Cor. 16:20; 2 Cor. 13:12; 1 Thess. 5:26; 1 Peter 5:14....[3]

[2]Merrill C. Tenney, ed., *The Zondervan Pictorial Bible Dictionary* (Grand Rapids: Zondervan, 1967), 432.

[3]William Smith, *Smith's Dictionary of the Bible*, rev. by F.N. and M.A. Peloubet (Nashville: Thomas Nelson, 1979), 338.

This explains a foreign custom that seemed quite natural for the early Christians, though it is strange to modern Americans. A Bible commentary may give you a brief explanation of this custom, but for further detail and for thorough Scripture cross referencing, you must turn to a Bible dictionary.

Suppose you read the passage in Paul's letters where he says, "I desire...that the women adorn themselves in modest apparel, with propriety and moderation, not with braided hair or gold or pearls or costly clothing" (1 Tim. 2:8-9). This spurs your curiosity. You wonder how stylish women did dress in Paul's time. The Bible commentary is not apt to elaborate at this point. A concordance will give little help, because relevant words like *make-up* or *jewelry* do not appear in Scripture. So you turn to a Bible encyclopedia, which contains not only Bible words but also topics not specifically mentioned in Scripture. There you read under the topic, *Make-Up*:

> From earliest times women have used beauty aids. In ancient Palestine, Egypt and Mesopotamia women put dark eyeshadow around their eyes. At first this was to protect their eyes against the strong sunshine. But it soon became a matter of fashion. The women used their fingers, spatulas made of wood or bronze, or fine brushes to put on their eyeshadow. And they had polished metal mirrors in which to study the effect![4]

This sort of fascinating information comes from ancient literature and from modern archaeological digs, which have uncovered actual cosmetics and cosmetic mirrors from biblical times. The specific article quoted here continues for about half a page, and the editors tell us that more details may be found under the encyclopedic headings of *Clothes-Making, Daily Life*, and *Dress*.

These three examples suggest some ways you might use a Bible dictionary or encyclopedia to fill in the gaps of your Bible knowledge. How can you determine which type of resource to use in a particular situation?

---

[4]Pat Alexander, ed., *Eerdmans' Concise Bible Encyclopedia* (Grand Rapids: William B. Eerdmans Publishing Company, 1980), 162.

What to Expect

Dictionaries and encyclopedias are not simply different names for the same thing. Each of these study aids has unique features.

A *dictionary* will list important words or phrases. It will explain their various meanings, their rootage in other words, and often their pronunciation. So a Bible dictionary attempts to list all the important words in the Bible, such as the proper names of people and places, terms for religious rites and customs, or doctrinal terms. It focuses on the Bible itself and does not attempt to define modern terms related to the Bible, such as the contemporary names of modern towns in Bible lands, post-biblical documents like the Dead Sea Scrolls, or technical methods of Bible criticism. When the Bible itself does not mention such things, the Bible dictionary does not. It is a repertory of actual Bible words and phrases.

An *encyclopedia*, on the other hand, is not limited to the words and phrases that appear in Scripture. It discusses anything that the editors feel might help our understanding of the Bible. Just as a secular encyclopedia covers the whole gamut of human learning—literature, history, philosophy, religion, biology, physics, etc.—a Bible encyclopedia touches all sorts of topics related to the Bible. Archaeology, military history, astrology and astronomy, ancient etiquette, and similar topics will appear in a Bible encyclopedia, even though the Bible may not explicitly refer to these subjects.

A Bible encyclopedia also discusses key topics from the Bible itself, such as important people and places. For example, here is a selected list of topics from the supplementary volume of *The Interpreter's Dictionary of the Bible,*[5] which is actually an encyclopedia:

Lachish	Lex Talionis
Láir	Libnah (city)
Laodicea	Lists, Ethical
Latin Versions	Literary Criticism
Law in the OT	Literature, The Bible As
Lectionary Cycle, Rabbinic	Literature, Early Christian
Letter	Liturgical Materials, NT
Leviticus	Lord

[5]Keith Grim, ed., *The Interpreter's Dictionary of the Bible,* suppl. vol. (Nashville: Abingdon Press, 1976).

As you can see, the encyclopedia contains some interesting topics that you would not find in a simple dictionary of Bible words. For this reason, it supplements the dictionary.

In either type of book, you should first expect to find a clear definition of each subject. If modern scholars are not sure of the meaning of a particular term, the writer should tell what is known of the subject instead of tossing out some ambiguous statement. Here is an example of a responsible treatment that concedes that much still is not known:

> **Unicorn**, the rendering of the Authorized Version of the Hebrew *rĕêm*, a word which occurs seven times in the Old Testament as the name of some large wild animal. The *rĕêm* of the Hebrew Bible, however, has nothing at all to do with the one-horned animal of the Greek and Roman writers, as is evident from Deut. 33:17.... Considering that the *rĕêm* is spoken of as a two-horned animal of great strength and ferocity, that it was evidently well-known and often seen by the Jews, that it is mentioned as an animal fit for sacrificial purposes, and that it is frequently associated with bulls and oxen, we think there can be no doubt that some species of wild ox is intended....[6]

While we do not conclusively know the meaning of some Bible terms such as *unicorn, behemoth,* or *leviathan,* a Bible dictionary or encyclopedia should clearly describe the meaning of biblical terms that are known, such as *cubit, Rephaim,* or *satrap.* Most English Bible versions do not attempt to explain these words, so you will need a Bible dictionary or encyclopedia to understand what they mean.

Second, you should expect this type of book to give a variety of Bible references to the term, if the Bible mentions it more than once. Here is an example of a place name that occurs again and again in Bible history, but you might overlook its various occurrences without the dictionary's list of Scripture references:

---

[6]Smith, *Dictionary of the Bible,* 720-21.

MEDEBA (*mêdᵉbā* possibly 'water of quiet'). A plain and city of Reuben (Jos. xiii. 9, 16) on the right side of the Amen. An old Moabite town taken from Moab by Sihon (Nu. xxi. 21-30), it was used by the Syrian allies of Ammon as a camping-site after their defeat at the hand of Joab (1 Ch. xix. 6-15).... It also figured in the history of the intertestamental era (1 Macc. ix. 36 ff. as 'Medaba'; Jos., *Ant.* i. .!4), before being captured by Hyrcanus after a long siege (Jos., *Ant.* xiii. 9.1).[7]

The foregoing example also illustrates the third important quality of a good Bible dictionary or encyclopedia: It should provide relevant information from ancient literature other than the Bible. The abbreviation *Jos., Ant.* in this example refers to Josephus' *Antiquities*, an important first-century history of the Jewish people. Other articles might mention the writings of Pliny, Marcus Aurelius, or other ancient authorities who shed light on Bible topics. This reference to ancient secular sources is a valuable feature.

Fourth, expect a good Bible dictionary or encyclopedia to convey the latest findings of archaeologists, linguists, and other Bible scholars. Publishers will issue periodic revisions of the book or bring out supplemental volumes to give their readers up-to-date information. A good case in point is the supplementary volumes of *The Interpreter's Dictionary of the Bible*. Issued decades after the first volumes came off the press, the supplements provide further information about topics such as the Hyksos of Egypt and the Gnostic "Gospels" of Nag Hammadi, based on recent findings.

Most Bible dictionaries and encyclopedias will attempt to describe the locations of Bible sites. Since the writers must rely on local Palestinian tradition or archaeological finds to pinpoint a site, and since archaeologists keep uncovering new data, they must move those map pins occasionally. Writers of the older Bible dictionaries, such as William Smith, could only guess at the locations of cities such as Ekron (Josh. 25:45-46) and Hazor (Josh. 11:1; 1 Kin. 9:15). However, excavations in the modern era have confirmed their locations.

---

[7]J.D. Douglas, ed., *The New Bible Dictionary* (Grand Rapids: William B. Eerdmans Publishing Company, 1962), 801.

Fifth, expect a good Bible dictionary or encyclopedia to mention any alternate names or spellings of a particular subject. Often a place name changed when foreign conquerors captured the site (e.g., Baal-Gad became "Paneas" under the Greeks and "Caesarea Philippi" under the Romans). Pagan deities were given various names (e.g., Nabu/Nebo or Merodach/Marduk) by their worshipers as the languages changed. Older English versions such as the KJV give archaic English names to objects that we know by different names today. Your Bible dictionary or encyclopedia should help you identify these alternate terms.

Finally, you should expect the book to have an efficient system of cross references to related topics. You will find the cross references listed as "See" or "See Also" notes, usually at the end of an article. A Bible dictionary article on *Philistines*, for example, might end by saying, "See also Caphtor, Joshua, Samson, and Saul." This directs you to further information about the Philistines under those headings.

How to Use these Aids

If you know the alphabet, you can use a Bible dictionary or encyclopedia. Finding things is just that simple—follow the alphabet to the topic you have in mind. After you have owned one of these books for awhile, you will be pleased to realize that you can use it...

- to find more detailed information about a Bible person or place
- to define the meaning of an obscure Bible term
- to follow the history of an ancient culture
- to research the origins of a Christian or Jewish doctrine
- to compare lifestyles in Bible times with modern lifestyles
- to visualize (with maps and other illustrations) what you are reading in the Bible
- to analyze a Bible book as literature (history, poetry, *apocalyptic literature*,* etc.)

The list might go on. No wonder so many pastors and Sunday school teachers like to take these books to their Bible classes! An educated person is not one who knows all the answers, but one who knows where to find them. The answers to many Bible questions can be found quickly in a good Bible dictionary or encyclopedia.

Bible Handbooks

Unlike Bible dictionaries or encyclopedias, which list articles in alphabetical order, the Bible handbook lists articles chronologically or according to the order of the books of the Bible (Genesis to Revelation). *Halley's Bible Handbook*, first published in 1924, is still the most popular reference book of this type.

Some Bible handbooks give a synopsis of each Bible book along with related items such as archaeological finds. (*Eerdmans' Handbook to the Bible* is an example.) Others emphasize the historical background to each book and provide only a minimal outline of the Scripture itself. (*Halley's* is an example.)

Although Bible handbooks are occasionally advertised as "encyclopedias," they must be less thorough than the Bible dictionary or encyclopedia can be. A certain amount of the text (sometimes the bulk of the book) must be devoted to summarizing the Bible narrative itself, so the writer can highlight only a few interesting facts from the scholars' store of knowledge.

For example, here is how one Bible handbook discusses the hostile relationship between Jews and Christians, which is a controversial topic among Bible scholars today:

> One of the more difficult areas to deal with is how relations with the Jews deteriorated throughout much of the NT [New Testament] period. Jesus himself was a Jew. Originally, of course, many Christians were Jews who accepted Jesus as the messiah. The Jewish leaders eventually expelled these people from the synagogue, probably around A.D. 90. After the fall of Jerusalem in A.D. 70 the Jews who escaped fled to Yavneh (also called Jamnia) and began to pull their lives together by collecting and organizing their scriptures. Christians did the same thing but fled to Pella (in the Jordan Valley). The NT shows that relations between these two groups in the wake of Jerusalem's destruction were sometimes highly volatile. Although this topic is quite complicated, I believe we must acknowledge its presence in the NT.

Later history saw the unfortunate development among Christians of anti-Semitism in an irrational and highly immoral way. It led ultimately to the terrible Holocaust (known to Jews as the Shoah) by the Nazis in World War II. I don't believe that the NT itself fosters this attitude intentionally, but excessive Christian interpretations throughout history led to these intolerable developments. When reading the NT, Christians should be careful not to use anachronistic labels.[8]

Hundreds of journal articles, dozens of books, and a multi-part television documentary by PBS have attempted to explain this crucial and complicated issue. A Bible handbook must deal with it in a single paragraph. Even with such tight space limitations, a Bible handbook's handy digest-style format appeals to many lay Bible students. They can read alongside the Bible itself, following the canonical order of the Bible books.

ANNOTATED BIBLIOGRAPHY

BIBLE DICTIONARIES

Achtemeier, Paul J. *Harper's Bible Dictionary*. New York: Harper, n.d.

Written with a liberal perspective, this dictionary gives useful background on the home life of Bible times, the geography and climate of Palestine, and other subjects of popular interest. Although brief on Bible history and theology, it might be used to supplement Unger's or Tenney's dictionaries, which are strong in those areas.

Hastings, James, ed. *A Dictionary of the Bible*, 5 vols. rev. F.C. Grant and H.H. Rowley. Peabody, MA: Hendrickson Publishers, 1989.

Hastings achieved an interesting blend of conservative and liberal scholarship on the staff of this project. Discoveries since this dictionary was first published (1898-1904) have left it outdated in some respects and the revisers have not fully solved this problem. But Hastings' dictionary still offers a good colloquy of liberal/

---

[8]Ronald D. Witherup, *The Bible Companion: A Handbook for Beginners* (New York: Crossroad Publishing, 1998), 165-66.

conservative views on Bible topics. Some of its articles (e.g., "Faith," "Predestination," "Sermon on the Mount") are among the best found anywhere. Hastings' work includes terms from the Apocrypha.

Mills, Watson E., gen. ed. *Mercer Dictionary of the Bible.* Macon, GA: Mercer University Press, 1990.

The National Association of Baptist Professors of Religion (NABPR) spearheaded this project, which was designed to be a reliable Bible dictionary for college and seminary students. Walter Harrelson, Carl F.H. Henry, G.R. Beasley-Murray, and other noted evangelical scholars appear among the contributors. While the dictionary's approach is conservative and traditional, it departs from the pattern of evangelical reference books in several respects. For example, it uses the Revised Standard Version (rejected by most evangelicals as being too liberal) as its scriptural basis. While the book is not graphically appealing, the articles do give useful background information for Bible study.

Smith, William. *Smith's Bible Dictionary*, rev. F.N. Peloubet and M.A. Peloubet. Nashville: Thomas Nelson, 1986.

Though one of the oldest Bible dictionaries, Smith's remains one of the most popular. Its articles are brief and informative,

Figure 16–Bible Handbook Entry, "The Festival Scrolls"

Ruth is one of the five books of the Hebrew Bible used by the Jews on particular feasts. They are called the *Megilloth*, or "festival scrolls." The five books and corresponding feasts are listed below.

Book of the Bible	Feast
Ruth	Pentecost
Song of Songs	Passover
Ecclesiastes	Tabernacles
Lamentations	Ninth of Ab
Esther	Purim

Source: Ronald D. Witherup, *The Bible Companion: A Handbook for Beginners* (New York: Crossroad, 1998), 72.

with a minimum of speculation. In fact, Barber thinks many of its articles are "unquestionably superior to similar articles in modern dictionaries" (ML, 44). The Peloubet revision takes account of important archaeological finds in the late 1800s, which other editions of Smith's dictionary do not.

Tenney, Merrill C., ed. *The Zondervan Pictorial Bible Dictionary*, rev. ed. Grand Rapids: Zondervan, 1988.

Tenney's articles are concise, meaty, and reliable. It is a good volume for quick reference. We should note that the book has several shortcomings. While it has numerous illustrations, many are of inferior quality. The bibliographies are of varying usefulness, and many major articles (e.g., "Resurrection of Jesus Christ") have no bibliography at all. Despite these deficiencies, Tenney's dictionary is a handy resource.

Unger, Merrill F. *Unger's Bible Dictionary*. Chicago: Moody Press, 1966.[9]

Dr. Unger revised *Barnes' Bible Encyclopedia*, an excellent work first published in 1913, to provide a more detailed discussion of key theological concepts and more up-to-date information on Bible sites. Many of Unger's articles (e.g., "Election" and "Sanctification") compare the doctrines of various Christian communions more succinctly than any other articles I have found. The photographs are good and the color maps are superb. With all things considered, this dictionary is one of the best.

BIBLE ENCYCLOPEDIAS

Alexander, Pat, ed. *Eerdmans' Concise Bible Encyclopedia*. Grand Rapids: William B. Eerdmans Publishing Company, 1981.

This book reorganizes the material of an immensely popular Bible handbook, *Eerdmans Family Encyclopedia of the Bible*, into alphabetical order. The articles are quite brief, Scripture references are sparse, and there are no bibliographies. However, the book's slim paperback format makes it easy to carry.

---

[9]Also available as *Unger's Concise Bible Dictionary* (Ada, MI: Baker Books, 1985) and *New Unger's Bible Dictionary* (Chicago: Moody Press, n.d.).

Bromiley, Geoffrey W., ed. *The International Standard Bible Encyclopedia*, rev. ed., 4 vols. Grand Rapids: William B. Eerdmans Publishing Company, 1995.

Here is a notable achievement by leading evangelical Bible scholars. The revised ISBE is even better than its well-acclaimed predecessor, which was published in 1939. The clearly outlined articles make its information easy to find, yet one can see the academic excellence and scholarly depth of every article. The bibliographies are quite good, though they often refer to out-of-print materials. The new ISBE rivals the *Interpreter's Dictionary* for thoroughness and usefulness.

Buttrick, George A., and Keith Grim, eds. *The Interpreter's Dictionary of the Bible*, 5 vols. Nashville: Abingdon Press, 1962-76.

This is surely the most exhaustive Bible encyclopedia of recent years. Nearly three hundred Christian and Jewish scholars collaborated on the IDB. Their work has a liberal viewpoint, and is thoroughly documented with journal articles and monographs of scholarly weight. The IDB puts a wealth of modern biblical research in the hands of any pastor or layman; it is an invaluable resource.

Packer, J.I., Merrill C. Tenney, and William White, Jr., eds. *Nelson's Illustrated Encyclopedia of Bible Facts*. Nashville: Thomas Nelson, 1995.

Having served as a project coordinator for the first edition of this book,[10] I may be accused of prejudice; but I believe it is the best one-volume Bible encyclopedia now available. Its forty-six articles (organized by subject in rough chronological order) discuss every major aspect of Bible culture and history; they are written with a conservative, evangelical perspective. The book contains over five hundred illustrations, many of which had not been published before. And its detailed index is superior to any I have seen in competing works.

---

[10]The book was first issued in 1980 under the title of *The Bible Almanac*. Nelson has reprinted it in various formats with various titles.

BIBLE HANDBOOKS

Alexander, David and Patricia. *Eerdmans' Handbook to the Bible*, rev. ed. Grand Rapids: William B. Eerdmans Publishing Company, 1983.

This colorful book summarizes Bible history in an entertaining and informative way, with related articles about recent archaeological finds concerning these events. The full-color photography is stunning and the maps are well-detailed.

Dowley, Tim and Peter Wyart, eds. *The Collegeville Bible Handbook*. Collegeville, MN: The Liturgical Press, 1997.

This handbook distills to one volume *The Collegeville Bible Commentary*, a popular-level Roman Catholic work based on the NAB. Lush full-color illustrations bring an eyewitness quality to the text. The *Handbook's* outlines are concise and easy to follow. Its maps lack detail and its index is disappointingly spare; but these features do not pose a great handicap for most study purposes.

Halley, Henry H. *Halley's Bible Handbook*. Grand Rapids: Zondervan, 1978.

Halley's book is the classic in this field, and this revised edition goes a long way toward updating its archaeological data. Halley cites many archaeological finds that confirm the authenticity of Bible history. He holds a conservative view of the authorship and dating of Bible books, and makes a good case for this view. The illustrations in this revision are also much better than in the original.

Hanke, Howard A. *The Thompson Chain-Reference Bible Companion*. Indianapolis: B.B. Kirkbride Bible Company, Inc., 1995.

This volume is actually a Bible handbook. Though Hanke gives us a perceptive introduction to each book of the Bible, he devotes the first one-third of his book to various articles on textual transmission, customs of Bible times, and major biblical themes. This conservative handbook has a detailed bibliography and index. A special feature is the Thompson-Chain numbering system in margin notes, which allows you to trace any article from Hanke's handbook to the topical chain of Thompson's famous study Bible.

Richards, Lawrence O. *Richard's Complete Bible Handbook*. Waco: Word, 1987.

Richards chooses to avoid discussing textual criticism and other academic matters. Instead, he narrates God's relationship with mankind as it progressed across the many centuries of Bible history. "For you and me, what is important when we read our Bible is not the debates of the scholars, but the wonderful realization that this Book is without question the authoritative, reliable, and relevant source of our faith," he explains. "It is God's Book, about Himself, and about us" (15). Richards' popularized style appeals to lay readers.

Unger, Merrill F. *New Unger's Bible Handbook*. Chicago: Moody Press, 1984.[11]

Barber calls this "the best work of its kind from the conservative point of view" (ML, 47), even ranking it ahead of *Halley's Bible Handbook*. Unger's book is truly superior in its handling of theological topics. The new edition has better eye appeal, by virtue of its new color illustrations. But it does not measure up to Halley's handbook in providing archaeological material of popular interest, nor is the style of writing on the level of Halley's or Richards' books.

Wiersbe, Warren W. *With the Word: A Chapter-by-Chapter Bible Handbook*. Nashville: Thomas Nelson, 1991.

A handy, economical reference book for laypersons, *With the Word* provides inspirational comment on the entire Bible. Wiersbe says it is designed to encourage the devotional reading of Scripture. One can readily see how it would do so. Wiersbe provides a capable pastoral guide through the pages of God's Word. Unlike other Bible handbooks, *With the Word* has no illustrations and little information about the insights of archaeology or classical studies. In spite of that, the book well accomplishes its goal of helping the reader live with the Word each day.

---

[11]Also available in a student edition (Chicago: Moody Press, 1998) and in Spanish from (Grand Rapids: Kregel Publications, 1987).

Willmington, H.L. *Willmington's Guide to the Bible*. Wheaton: Tyndale House, 1981.

Dr. Willmington summarizes the content of each book of the Bible and draws out the chief spiritual lessons to be learned from it. His archaeological information is not very deep or current and there are no illustrations. The book seems designed to be a teacher's resource rather than a personal study resource.

Witherup, Ronald D. *The Bible Companion: A Handbook for Beginners*. New York: Crossroad, 1998.

Father Witherup here gives us a friendly, inviting guide to the entire Bible, covering the Apocrypha as well as the usual books of the Protestant canon. While he is a respected Roman Catholic lecturer, he does not attempt to teach Catholic dogma here. Each chapter begins with a sidebar that gives a "bird's-eye view" of the Bible book under study, including the date, authorship, and outline. Father Witherup does not discuss higher-critical theories and other academic issues. *The Bible Companion* has no photos or other illustrations; however, the text is clearly written and substantive.

Chapter 8

Bible Atlases

Atlas was the mythical Greek god who was condemned to carry the world on his shoulders. So it was a stroke of advertising genius when seventeenth-century map publisher Gerard Mercator printed a sketch of this god on the frontispiece of his global map collection, with the title: *Atlas, or a Geographical Description of the World.*

That was in 1636. Few people today remember the name Mercator, but the name of *Atlas* is applied to almost every popular collection of maps.

A reliable Bible atlas is a prized possession of the Bible student. It helps the reader visualize where biblical events took place. A good Bible atlas demonstrates where the Israelites traveled in their wilderness wanderings, or Jesus on His Galilean preaching tour, or Paul on his missionary exploits. A Bible atlas with relief markings (lines or shadings that show the contours of the land) portrays land features that figure prominently in Bible history, such as the rugged terrain where Amos lived or the arid desert lowlands around the Dead Sea.

The better Bible atlases contain a *gazetteer*,* which lists significant towns, rivers, and other features with code numbers to help you locate them on the maps. A gazetteer may also provide the pronunciation of place names. All of these features can save you a great deal of research time.

A few atlases have articles about the geography and climate of Palestine, perhaps with rainfall and temperature charts to give some idea of how the climate of the Holy Land compares to your own. Some review the major events of Bible history in a given region. The newer atlases have photographs showing how Bible sites look today.

Keep in mind that we do not know exactly where many Bible sites were. Even when we do know the locations (thanks to archaeologists' findings), the mapmakers may not show the information accurately because they are accustomed to working with modern geographical data. In their line of work, they often must redraw political boundaries, change the names of or countries, and show minute geographical changes caused by earthquakes and the like. But seldom do they need to plot the locations of cities that disappeared several millennia ago—except when they are drawing Bible maps.[1]

When a modern mapmaker draws a diagram of the biblical world, the only means of checking the work is to consult some other bewildered artist's Bible map. The mapmaker must let archaeologists and textual scholars judge its accuracy, because no one else can. He could put Pittsburgh on the wrong side of the Susquehanna River and millions of people would notice it. But if he put Beth-shan on the wrong side of the Jordan, few would notice and fewer would correct him.

A noted authority on Bible geography, Denis Baly, says the problem of inaccurate Bible maps is much more common than we may realize. While reviewing a well-known Bible atlas, he groaned that its accuracy was "…deplorable. It has Petra in three different places, none of them the right one, Ctesiphon in two places, and so on. It even has the Dead Sea misplaced on one map."[2]

Even with this caution about the errors it's likely to contain, I encourage you to obtain a Bible atlas. In spite of its inaccuracies, an atlas will give you a better understanding of the Bible narrative than you could obtain by using your imagination.

What to Expect

Expect any good Bible atlas to include maps from various eras of biblical history. One basic map for the Old Testament and one for the New (with minor rescrambling of boundaries and place names) are not enough.

For example, the atlas should show the spread of early civilizations across the Fertile Crescent of Mesopotamia before the time of Abraham. It should show the route of the Israelites' wilder-

---

[1] I am oversimplifying the mapmaker's work in order to make a point. A professional mapmaker, a cartographer, will describe the task of revising a map as much more complicated than this.

[2] Denis Baly, "What to Look for in a Biblical Atlas," *The Biblical Archaeologist* (Winter 1982), 61. He is describing the *Rand McNally Bible Atlas* by E.G.H. Kraeling (New York: Rand McNally, 1956), now out of print.

ness journey from Egypt to Canaan. It might even show the stages of their conquest of Canaan. Certainly, it should show the tribal divisions of the land after the Conquest. The atlas should show how the land was divided by the rival nations of Israel and Judah after King Solomon.

Expect New Testament maps to show the Roman provinces of Jesus' day, Jesus' travels in Judea, and Paul's missionary journeys. The omission of any of these maps will hinder your study of the Bible.

You should expect a good Bible atlas to name the rivers, mountains, and other major geographical features in Bible history. This should go without saying, but several Bible atlases do not name such features, except for the Mediterranean Sea or the Jordan River.

Of course, the degree of detail will vary from one atlas to another. Some name only the major cities such as Jerusalem, Bethel, and Tyre, yet omit the smaller (but important) towns such as Gilgal, Emmaus, and Sidon.

Look for names of Roman provinces on any New Testament map of the Mediterranean world. With these identified, you will know what the Book of Acts means when it refers to areas such as Dalmatia, Achaia, or Pamphilia.

The best atlases also delineate major trade routes. This demonstrates that Palestine was an important crossroad in the ancient world and a military prize that often attracted surrounding military powers such as Egypt and Assyria.

Finally, the best atlases include charts and/or maps of rainfall. Because Palestine is largely an arid region, the people depend on regular rains or snows for their survival. When people of Bible times failed to get adequate rains for several seasons, they had severe famine. Baly writes, "In view of the tremendous importance of rainfall in the life of the Israelites and surrounding peoples, it is surprising how little attention is given in biblical atlases to climate."[3] Fortunately, the newest atlases provide this information.

---

[3]Baly, 62.

How to Use a Bible Atlas

Advice about the use of a Bible atlas is difficult to give, because each book is laid out in its own way. Perhaps these general suggestions will be of some help:

1. Remember that the city or feature you are trying to locate may have several names. In Chapter 7, I pointed out that a good Bible dictionary or encyclopedia should give you this information. For example, you may not be able to locate "Zion" in a Bible atlas, but your Bible dictionary will explain that "Zion" is another name for Jerusalem.

Using an atlas with a Bible dictionary or encyclopedia will also help you locate lesser-known places that may not be shown on a Bible map at all. A good example would be the Mount Salmon (or Zalmon) mentioned in Psalm 68:14. I know of no Bible atlas that shows it; but *Smith's Bible Dictionary* suggests that, in light of another reference in Judges 9:48, it must be "a hill near Shechem."[4] The Bible atlas will show you where Shechem is.

2. Beware of several sites with duplicate names. For example, the Old Testament describes two cities named "Bethel" and at least three cities named "Gibeah." Consult a Bible dictionary or encyclopedia to learn about such duplicate names, so you can locate the particular city you are trying to find.

3. Be sure to consult the proper map for the period of history you are studying. This seems elementary, but it may require some careful thought. Finding Tekoa, Amos' home town, requires using a map of Palestine after the Israelite conquest. In order to find Caesarea while you are studying Paul's travels, you must consult a New Testament map of Palestine—and then you must know which Caesarea you want to locate, because there were two. The Bible dictionary or encyclopedia will tell you when the city was established, and the map *legend** will tell what period is covered by the map.

4. Compare the scale of a Bible map to that of a map of an area you know, in order to get an idea of relative sizes and distances. Many Americans assume that Palestine is much larger than it really is. After all, we reason, so many significant events have occurred

---

[4]William Smith, *Smith's Bible Dictionary*, rev. F.N. and M.A. Peloubet (Nashville: Thomas Nelson, 1979), 581.

there and the country is displayed on a full-page map, as we are accustomed to seeing the United States displayed. But Palestine is actually about the size of New Hampshire. "From Dan to Beersheba" (Judg. 20:1) was about half the distance from New York to Washington, D.C.

5. Keep a supply of tracing paper in your atlas, since a Bible map must combine many eras of history onto one page. A map of Palestine in Old Testament times, for example, must show the cities built during more than two thousand years. You can use a piece of tracing paper to "lift off" the key cities you are studying, or to trace the travels of a Bible character without being distracted by irrelevant details.

Study Bibles, reference Bibles, and other reference books often have good sets of Bible maps in them. (The map and gazetteer in *The New Oxford Annotated Bible* are the best I've seen.) But such compact map sets can seldom offer the detail and depth of information that a full-fledged Bible atlas contains. It is worth having one to aid your study.

ANNOTATED BIBLIOGRAPHY

This list also includes Bible geographies, which describe the geography of Palestine, often with some supplementary maps. These books are so closely related to atlases that it seemed fitting to list them here.

ATLASES

Aharoni, Yohanan, and Michael Avi-Yonah. *The Macmillan Bible Atlas*, rev. ed. New York: Macmillan Publishing Company, 1993.

Providing a different map for every major event of Bible history (264 maps in all), *The Macmillan Bible Atlas* is one of the most interesting to read straight through. It is not as colorfully illustrated as some. The map captions are sometimes difficult to read, nor does the atlas show as many of the small Bible cities as one would like. But it does offer the best sequential review of Bible history that I have found in a Bible atlas.

Dowley, Tim, ed. *Atlas of the Bible and Christianity*. Ada, MI: Baker Books, 1997.

Dazzling full-color maps and photographs unfold the history of the Bible and the growth of Christianity from the first century to modern times. Dowley and his team of researchers have assembled a most attractive and thorough reference book, which deserves a place in every library where careful Bible study is done. Students of church history will appreciate the maps that explain the spread of great religious movements in the Western world, including the interaction between Christianity and Islam.

Pfeiffer, Charles F. *Baker's Bible Atlas*, rev. ed. Ada, MI: Baker Books, 1962.

The gazetteer in this volume is excellent and up-to-date. It identifies biblical sites by their modern names as well as their biblical names, which helps the reader to follow news of current archaeological finds in these areas. The maps are fairly detailed, though they are not as colorful as some in other atlases.

Wright, G. Ernest, and Floyd V. Filson. *The Westminster Historical Maps of Bible Lands*. Louisville: Westminster John Knox Press, 1952.

This atlas offers a strong combination of features—informative text, detailed maps (95 in all), and a good gazetteer. Wright and Filson assign dates to some Bible events (such as the Exodus) that conservative readers will question. But their narrative of Bible history is clear and generally dependable.

GEOGRAPHIES

Aharoni, Yohanan. *The Land of the Bible*, trans. A.F. Rainey. Louisville: Westminster John Knox Press, 1980.

Aharoni is one of the foremost Israeli scholars of today. This book and his *Macmillan Bible Atlas* reflect his masterful knowledge of Palestine. Aharoni describes key events of the intertestamental period, such as the Maccabean Revolt, which will be of special interest to students of the Apocrypha. He scarcely refers to New Testament events, however.

Baly, Denis A. *Basic Biblical Geography*. Minneapolis: Augsburg Fortress Press, 1987.

Baly's work is a standard textbook at many Christian colleges. The illustrations are not as clear or colorful as those found in other atlases or geographies, but this shortcoming is more than offset by Baly's superior knowledge of Palestinian geography. He describes not only topography but also the botany, meteorology, and other aspects of the Holy Land closely tied to its geography.

Chapter 9

Bible Surveys and Introductions

When a college student takes an introductory course in Bible, the textbook will be a Bible survey or introduction. Surprisingly, very few laymen know that these books are available.

As its name implies, a Bible *survey** is a "walking tour" through the Bible, citing the points of interest and showing how various parts of the Scripture are related to one another. A Bible *introduction** sets forth the chief theological themes of the Bible, such as the theme of redemption. So while the Bible survey summarizes Scripture, the Bible introduction analyzes Scripture. While the survey is for beginning students, the introduction is for more advanced students.

Because Bible surveys give you an overview of Bible history, they can help you get your bearings as a beginning Bible student. When you understand the story of God's dealings with mankind, you will be ready to delve into the Bible's doctrinal teachings, which the Bible introduction can help you to do.

Not a Casual Exercise

The simplicity of these books leads some people to think they can read straight through them, as they might read a Bible handbook. But that's not wise. Though simple in format, a Bible survey or introduction is packed with substantial information.

Let's consider two examples. Here is a brief quotation from Samuel J. Schultz's excellent book, *The Old Testament Speaks*. It's found in the chapter entitled, "Fading Hopes of Davidic Kings":

> Zedekiah was under constant pressure to join the Egyptians in a rebellion against Babylon. When Psammetichus II succeeded Necho (594), Edom, Moab, Ammon, and Phoenicia joined Egypt in an anti-Babylonian coalition, creating a crisis in Judah. With a wooden yoke around his neck Jeremiah dramatically announced that Nebuchadnezzar was God's servant to

whom the nations should willingly submit. Zedekiah was assured that submission to the Babylonian king would avert the destruction of Jerusalem (Jer. 27).[1]

Now here is an excerpt from Edward J. Young's book, An *Introduction to the Old Testament*, discussing the same period of Bible history:

...[Jeremiah] 27, although dated (verse 1) in the beginning of the reign of Jehoiakim, belongs, as its context shows, to the reign of Zedekiah. The chapter shows how the prophet thwarted the designs of five neighbouring peoples, Edom, Moab, Ammon, Tyre, Zidon (verse 2), to induce the Judean king to unite with them in a rebellion against Babylon. Jeremiah further spoke to Zedekiah about the folly of such action (verses 12-22).[2]

Dr. Schultz's book is a Bible survey; Dr. Young's is a Bible introduction. Dr. Schultz summarizes the impact of the yoke prophecy upon the prophetic career of Jeremiah himself, upon the politics of Zedekiah, and upon the survival of Judah as a nation. But Dr. Young analyzes this passage in the Book of Jeremiah to show how the yoke prophecy furthered the message of Jeremiah's prophetic ministry.

Such articles may entice you to engage in a further study of Zedekiah and his rebellion against Babylon. You might look up the word *yoke* in an exhaustive concordance and find the exact Scripture passage where Jeremiah's yoke prophecy is recorded (Jer. 27:1-14). Or you might turn to an article on Zedekiah in a Bible dictionary and read more about the king's life, as in this excerpt from *Smith's Bible Dictionary*:

It is evident that Zedekiah was a man not so much bad at heart as weak in will. It is evident from Jer. 27 and 28 that the earlier portion of Zedekiah's reign was marked by an agitation throughout the whole of Syria against the Babylonian yoke. Jerusalem seems to have taken the lead, since in the fourth year of Zedekiah's reign we find

---

[1] Samuel J. Schultz, *The Old Testament Speaks*, 3rd ed. (New York: Harper, 1980), 227.

[2] Edward J. Young, *An Introduction to the Old Testament*, rev. ed. (Grand Rapids: William B. Eerdmans Publishing Company, 1964), 237.

ambassadors from all the neighboring kingdoms—Tyre, Sidon, Edom, and Moab—at his court to consult as to the steps to be taken. The first act of rebellion of which any record survives was the formation of an alliance with Egypt....[3]

You could also consult articles on Necho, Egypt, or Jeremiah in a Bible dictionary, or check on Psammetichus II in a Bible handbook or encyclopedia. You could read an expository commentary on Jeremiah 27 for further background information. The Bible survey or introduction is simply your first step toward using all of these research avenues to better understand the Scripture itself.

Higher Criticism

As with commentaries, questions about higher criticism will arise when you use Bible surveys or introductions. In fact, some authors of these books take the opportunity to argue for their own higher-critical theories in great detail, citing passages of Scripture that illustrate their views.

A good example is Charles A. Briggs' *General Introduction to the Holy Scriptures*. Briggs was an early liberal proponent of source criticism, and he explores this theme throughout his book. Donald Guthrie's *New Testament Introduction* is a more recent example, in which a conservative scholar employs various methods of higher criticism, too. If you are aware of the methods that such writers use to analyze Scripture and discuss Bible history, you can understand why they disagree. This awareness also helps you evaluate a particular writer's view more carefully.

How to Use these Aids

Bible surveys and introductions come in so many different formats that it is impossible to give a simple set of guidelines for using them. Be sure to notice the special features of each book in the preface. Here are some general tips that might help you:

1. *Keep a concordance and Bible dictionary close at hand while using a Bible survey or introduction.* The example from Jeremiah 27 shows how these other reference books might supplement your

---

[3]William Smith, *Smith's Bible Dictionary*, ed. by F.N. and M.A. Peloubet (Nashville: Thomas Nelson, 1979), 760.

reading. The Bible survey or introduction paints the broad out-lines, while other reference books will sketch in the details.

2. *Use a current Bible encyclopedia to update the archaeological data.* Many old Bible surveys and introductions are still in print, and new archaeological finds may alter what authors have said about the military, political, or cultural background of a given event. If the publication date of such a book is more than ten years old, be sure to check its statements against a more recent Bible encyclopedia.

3. *Use the index.* A well-constructed index can guide you through the book. For example, Merrill C. Tenney defines and describes the Greek philosophy of Epicureanism in the opening chapter of his *New Testament Survey.*[4] A quick glance at the index tells you that he discusses it again, this time in the full context of Paul's speech on Mars' Hill, on page 286 of that volume. Since a Bible survey or introduction generally proceeds through the Bible book by book, you may need to use its index to track down all the references to a given subject that interests you.

ANNOTATED BIBLIOGRAPHY

In this list, I have also included several Bible histories because they serve basically the same function as Bible surveys.

INTRODUCTIONS AND SURVEYS

Anderson, Bernhard W. *Understanding the Old Testament*, 3rd ed. Paramus, NJ: Prentice-Hall, 1986.

Anderson's popular introduction examines the major theolog-ical themes of the Old Testament, such as covenant-making and vicarious sacrifice. The text is easy to understand and the illustrations are crisp. Along the way, Anderson explains the documentary hypothesis of the Pentateuch, form criticism of the Psalms, and other higher-critical concerns. He has a liberal perspective.

---

[4]Merrill C. Tenney, *New Testament Survey* (Grand Rapids: William B. Eerd-mans Publishing Company, 1961), 76-78.

Archer, Gleason L. *A Survey of Old Testament Introduction*, rev. ed. Chicago: Moody Press, 1996.[5]

Dr. Archer is a professor at Trinity Evangelical Divinity School who has won wide recognition as a conservative Old Testament scholar. Barber applauds this introduction as "a definitive study which takes its place among the front rank of works in the field..." (ML, 81).

Brown, Raymond E. *An Introduction to the New Testament*. New York: Doubleday, 1997.

During his teaching career at Union Theological Seminary, Dr. Brown earned a reputation as one of the foremost New Testament scholars of America. Yet he had an extraordinary ability to communicate biblical teaching in intriguing ways that the laity could understand. In this *Introduction*, Father Brown takes us on a book-by-book tour of the New Testament. However, he does more than review the message of Scripture. He answers many questions that today's readers have about the Bible. He responds helpfully to controversial ideas that have been advanced by the Jesus Seminar and other revisionist scholars. Dr. Brown brings a conservative Roman Catholic perspective to these issues.

Childs, Brevard. *Introduction to the Old Testament as Scripture*. Minneapolis: Augsburg Fortress Press, 1979.

Using a higher-critical method now popular in Europe, called *canon criticism*,* Professor Childs attempts to show how Jews of the intertestamental era selected the writings that we now consider to be Scripture. He seeks to demonstrate that the Old Testament is a product of the Judeo-Christian tradition as much as it is a source of that tradition.

Feine, Paul, Johannes Behm, and Werner Georg Kümmel, *Introduction to the New Testament*, trans. Howard C. Kee, rev. ed. Nashville: Abingdon Press, 1996.

This introduction shows at length the kinds of information that higher-critical methods can uncover in the New Testament. The authors are leading German champions of higher-critical Bible

---

[5]Also available as *Resena Critica de una Introduccion al Antiguo Testamento* (Grand Rapids: Kregel Publications, 1982).

study. Their book is sophisticated and often bewildering, especially in their discussion of the Gospels. It is meant for the advanced Bible student.

Gantt, Michael. *A NonChurchgoer's Guide to the Bible*. Intercourse, PA: Good Books, 1995.

Michael Gantt is a Christian businessman and former pastor, who sets before us "a user-friendly, nonsectarian introduction" to the Bible. Gantt uses plain language that anyone can understand, without patronizing the reader. He invites the reader to explore the Bible to find out what God's Word says, yet he avoids doctrinal controversy. He describes the various parts of the Bible with balance and engaging interest. Chapters 5-10 comprise a handy layman's survey of all the books of the Bible.

Gundry, Robert H., *A Survey of the New Testament*, rev. ed. Grand Rapids: Zondervan, 1994.

Dr. Gundry's survey has been a standard textbook in evangelical colleges since its first publication in 1970. Outline headings printed in the margin help the reader find comments on every significant New Testament passage. Dr. Gundry's outlines are well worth the price of the entire *Survey*.

Guthrie, Donald. *New Testament Introduction*, rev. ed. Downers Grove, IL: InterVarsity, 1990.

Wiersbe terms this Bible survey "essential" (BLBS, 17). Guthrie makes a solid case for the conservative view of scriptural inspiration as he reviews the seeming discrepancies in the Gospels and other matters that trouble first-time readers of the New Testament.

Harrison, Everett F. *Introduction to the New Testament*. Grand Rapids: William B. Eerdmans Publishing Company, 1971.

Here is another excellent conservative survey of the New Testament. Harrison does not resolve the Synoptic problem as well as Guthrie, and he seems to avoid some difficult issues that other survey writers have tackled. But his treatment is clear and easy to follow.

Harrison, Roland K. *Introduction to the Old Testament.* Grand Rapids: William B. Eerdmans Publishing Company, 1969.

No other North American scholar has created a volume of such depth and comprehensiveness. Harrison ably describes the liberal and conservative viewpoints of crucial issues in biblical criticism (e.g., his sections on the authorship of the Psalms and Isaiah). Yet he consistently espouses the more traditional and conservative view. The book's only weakness is its superficial subject index.

Hiebert, D. Edmond. *An Introduction to the New Testament,* 3 vols. Winona Lake, IN: BMH Publishing, 1954-75.

Former professor of New Testament at Mennonite Brethren Seminary in Fresno, CA, Dr. Hiebert approaches this work with a conservative yet non-sectarian attitude. He addresses the more serious layperson or pastor, with a thoughtful review of each major section of the New Testament. His treatment of Revelation avoids speculation and challenges the reader to further study.

LaSor, William Sanford, David Allan Hubbard, and Frederic William Bush. *Old Testament Survey.* Grand Rapids: William B. Eerdmans Publishing Company, 1996.

The authors attempt to employ modern techniques of literary criticism while respecting the divine authority of the Scriptures. The result is a moderate and well-balanced survey. Liberal readers will not like the authors' caution in matters of textual criticism, while conservative readers may feel they are too concerned with literary genres. However, the survey is worthy of respect. It is carefully reasoned, thoroughly footnoted, and attractively illustrated.

Ramsay, William M. *The Westminster Guide to the Books of the Bible.* Louisville: Westminster John Knox Press, 1994.

Former professor of religion at Bethel College, a Presbyterian school in Mackenzie, TN, Dr. Ramsay wrote the *Layman's Guide to the New Testament* in 1981. This new book expands the *Layman's Guide* to encompass the entire Bible, including the Apocrypha. Dr. Ramsay assumes the reader is not well-versed in the theories of biblical criticism, yet he leads the reader into those technical issues by introducing the concepts gradually and methodically. Dr.

Ramsay gives us an ecumenical introduction to the books of the Bible, explaining the differences between Catholic, Orthodox, and Protestant interpretations of Scripture with even-handed skill.

Schultz, Samuel J. *The Old Testament Speaks*, 3rd ed. San Francisco: Harper San Francisco, 1990.

The most simply written Old Testament survey I have found, Dr. Schultz's book is nonetheless full of useful information about the military, political, and religious influences of nations that affected ancient Israel. His book shows a good acquaintance with the newly discovered historical records of Assyria, Babylon, and other ancient cultures. Dr. Shultz taught Old Testament at Wheaton College.

Tenney, Merrill C. *New Testament Survey*, rev. ed. Grand Rapids: William B. Eerdmans Publishing Company, 1985.

This is the basic textbook for the introductory course in New Testament at many evangelical schools. Dr. Tenney provides a clear narration of New Testament events. He also sketches in interesting background details, such as the Greek and Roman philosophies of that day, the Jewish sects and political parties, and so on. The maps and other illustrations are well executed.

Wilkinson, Bruce, and Kenneth Boa. *Talk through the Bible*. Nashville: Thomas Nelson, 1983.

Thousands of Christian laypersons are acquainted with Mr. Wilkinson's "Walk Through the Bible" seminars, which teach the content of various Bible books with a clever system of hand signals and other mnemonic devices. This Bible introduction offers a more detailed treatment of each Bible book. It is dispensational and premillennial in its handling of prophetic books such as Daniel and Revelation.

HISTORIES

Bright, John. *A History of Israel*, 3rd ed. Louisville: Westminster John Knox Press, 1981.

A former professor at Union Theological Seminary, Richmond, Bright recounts Israel's history with scholarly depth and flair. He brings a liberal perspective to critical matters (e.g., he identifies two authors of Isaiah). His comparison of Israel's religion to the pagan religions of her neighbors is still unsurpassed.

Bruce, F.F. *New Testament History*. Garden City, NY: Doubleday, 1972.

Dr. Bruce covers the history recorded in New Testament Scripture as well as the attendant history recorded in secular sources such as Josephus. This book is prized by beginning New Testament students because it digests so much vital information for them. More advanced students appreciate Bruce's conservative treatment of the dates of Jesus' ministry, the significance of the Book of Revelation, and other controversial issues.

Wood, Leon J. and David O'Brien, *A Survey of Israel's History*. Grand Rapids: Zondervan, 1986.

This conservative study of Old Testament history is not as detailed as Bright's book, yet it is an excellent guide for the beginner. Pastors and Sunday School teachers can easily use it for their own "refresher course" in Old Testament history.

Chapter 10

Miscellaneous Resources

The purpose of *Swords & Whetstones* is to introduce a broad range of Bible study resources. However, some valuable resources do not fit any of the categories we have examined so far. This brief chapter introduces a novel assortment of such Bible reference books. If you have not found the type of study aid you were hoping for in the first nine chapters, you may very well find it here.[1]

Analyses and Outlines

Books in this category give you a simple review of the Bible story. They retrace Bible history, beginning with God's creation of all things in Genesis and climaxing with God's final redemption of His chosen people in the Book of Revelation. Some of these books also discuss the progressive development of humanity's relationship with God—the various covenants of mercy, dispensations of God's will, and so on.

These books are useful in deductive Bible study (the "telescope" method). They give you a panorama of a certain Bible book or of the Bible as a whole, before you begin analyzing its various parts. Turn to a book like this for a quick review of certain biblical events, doctrines, or ideas as you prepare a Sunday school lesson or Bible study. (In this case, it's best to select a book with a good index.)

Harmonies

In the late 1800s, as German scholars began pointing out the *Synoptic problem,** several editors compiled Gospel harmonies. They laid out in parallel columns the related passages from the three Synoptic Gospels. This allowed readers to compare how Matthew, Mark, and Luke recorded the same incident or teaching.

---

[1]Remember that we have omitted technical reference books, such as lexicons and interlinear Bibles, because our goal is to help laypersons find the tools they need for everyday Bible study.

Figure 17–A Gospel Harmony of the Baptism of Jesus (NKJV)

Matthew 3:13-16	Mark 1:9-11	Luke 3:21-23	John 1:29-33
Then Jesus came from Galilee to John at the Jordan to be baptized by him. And John tried to prevent Him, saying, "I need to be baptized by You, and You are coming to me?" But Jesus answered and said to him, "Permit it to be so now, for thus it is fitting for us to fulfill all righteousness." Then he allowed Him. When He had been baptized, Jesus came up immediately from the water, and behold, the heavens were opened to Him, and He saw the Spirit of God descending like a dove and alighting upon Him. And suddenly a voice came from heaven, saying, "This is My beloved Son, in whom I am well pleased."	It came to pass in those days that Jesus came from Nazareth to Galilee, and was baptized by John in the Jordan. And immediately, coming up from the water, He saw the heavens parting and the Spirit descending upon Him like a dove. Then a voice came from heaven, "You are My beloved Son, in whom I am well pleased."	When all the people were baptized, it came to pass that Jesus also was baptized, and while He prayed, the heaven was opened. And the Holy Spirit descending in bodily form like a dove upon Him, and a voice came from heaven which said, "You are My beloved Son; in You I am well pleased."	The next day John saw Jesus coming toward him, and said, "Behold! The Lamb of God who takes away the sin of the world! This is He of whom I said, 'After me comes a man who is preferred before me, for He was before me.' I did not know Him; but that He should be revealed to Israel, therefore I came baptizing with water." And John bore witness, saying, "I saw the Spirit descending from heaven like a dove, and He remained upon Him. I did not know Him, but He who sent me to baptize with water said to me, 'Upon whom you see the Spirit descending and remaining on Him, this is He who baptizes with the Holy Spirit.' And I have seen and testified that this is the Son of God."

The Gospel accounts of Jesus' baptism have several similarities, but notice their differences. Mark and Luke say that Jesus heard the voice from heaven, saying, "You are My beloved Son." They suggest that the voice affirmed Jesus' identity to himself. Matthew and John record that the voice spoke to others, saying, "This is My beloved Son." John notes the word of John the Baptist, who said that God used the dove and the voice to confirm to him personally who Jesus was.

It permitted anyone to test the higher critics' theories of how the Synoptics had been written.

A flurry of Gospel harmonies came from the presses around the turn of the century, but only a few have survived. The best harmonies are the ones with good *critical apparatus,** such as footnotes showing alternate English readings and variant Greek readings.

Ambitious modern researchers have compiled other types of Bible harmonies—harmonies of the Synoptics and the Gospel of John, harmonies of the events in Paul's life, and so on. However, the Synoptic harmonies are still the most popular. You can use a Gospel harmony for two basic purposes: (1) to understand the Synoptic problem, or (2) to obtain information that is missing from a particular Gospel account, by seeing how the other Gospel writers record that event.

Chronologies

Ever since Bishop Ussher attempted to lay out a chronology of the Bible (see Chapter 2), Bible students have retraced his steps through the Bible records. They have tried to fix the exact calendar dates of momentous events such as the Exodus from Egypt or the crucifixion of Christ. Some scholars have published weighty monographs on this subject; others have penned colorful studies for more popular consumption. The fact remains that we cannot absolutely determine the dates of Bible events in terms of our modern calendar.

Are the Old Testament genealogies complete? Do they overlap? Do they soar into *hyperbole** at some points? Scholars have made some noble attempts to solve these riddles of Bible chronology. Use them with discretion, mindful of the limits of contemporary scholarship.

Character Studies

One fascinating form of deductive Bible study is the character study. In this method, you garner relevant Scripture passages about a Bible character in order to learn all you can about that figure's personality, thoughts, and activities. This can be very informative. For example, did you know that Moses had more than one wife? Or that Peter was married? Or that Jesus fed four thousand and five thousand people, on two separate occasions? Studying the life of a Bible character will uncover many such little-known facts.

Several authors have already done the research for you. They have compiled books on the lives of Jesus, Peter, Paul, and other prominent biblical people. Perhaps the best-known writer of character studies is Herbert Lockyer, whose popular Bible character series has included *All the Men of the Bible* (1958), *All the Kings and Queens of the Bible* (1961), *All the Women of the Bible* (1979), *All the Children of the Bible* (1979), and *All the Apostles of the Bible* (1979).

Archaeological Studies

Archaeologists keep digging up so much information about the world of the Bible that publishers can scarcely keep the reference books up to date! Also, there are a number of new books about biblical archaeology itself—its purpose, its methods, and its important discoveries. These archaeological studies will enable you to use other Bible reference books with more discretion. They will alert you to statements in those resources that must be revised in light of recent discoveries in this field.

Early twentieth-century archaeologists W.F. Albright, James B. Pritchard, and G. Ernest Wright wrote some classic books on this subject. They are not included in the bibliography because their work is dated. Even so, you may wish to consult them for some interesting background on the methods archaeologists have used, and for their speculations about early finds in the Holy Land.[2]

ANNOTATED BIBLIOGRAPHY
ANALYSES AND OUTLINES

Baxter, J. Sidlow. *Explore the Book.* Grand Rapids: Zondervan, 1986.

Baxter's popular style makes this Bible summary useful to anyone. Baxter is conservative, evangelical, and devotional in his

---

[2]Especially see W.F. Albright, *Archaeology of Palestine* (Magnolia, MA: Peter Smith Publisher, 1990); James B. Pritchard, ed., *The Ancient Near East in Pictures* (Princeton: Princeton University Press, 1969); James B. Pritchard, *Ancient Near Eastern Texts Relating to the Old Testament* (Princeton: Princeton University Press, 1969).

approach to Scripture. He has a real gift for singling out the main theological theme of each book and expressing it in a simple way.

Lee, Robert. *Outline Studies in John.* Grand Rapids: Kregel Publications, 1987.[3]

Presented in convenient chart form, these outlines of Bible books are a helpful aid to personal or group Bible study. A concise introduction to each book runs across the top of each outline page.

Mears, Henrietta C. *What the Bible Is All About.* rev. ed. Ventura, CA.: Regal, 1997.

This synopsis of Bible doctrine from an evangelical point of view is especially helpful to beginning Bible students. The author shows how Scripture presents great spiritual truths, such as humanity's redemption from sin, in both Old and New Testaments. She develops well the concept of progressive revelation.[4]

Scroggie, W. Graham. *The Unfolding Drama of Redemption.* Grand Rapids: Kregel Publications, 1995.

This conservative British writer focuses on humanity's redemption as the principal theme of Scripture, showing how every book of the Bible develops that theme. It is a fascinating study.

HARMONIES

The Bethany Parallel Commentary. Minneapolis: Bethany House Publishers, 1983.[5]

This massive volume gives the commentaries of Matthew Henry, Jamieson-Fausset-Brown, and Adam Clarke in parallel columns. Notes from Charles H. Spurgeon, Albert Barnes, Martin

---

[3]Other volumes in this series include *Outline Studies in Acts* (Grand Rapids: Kregel Publications, 1987); *Outline Studies in Romans* (Grand Rapids: Kregel Publications, 1989); and *Outline Studies in Galatians* (Grand Rapids: Kregel Publications, 1979)

[4]Also available as *What the Bible Is All About* (Wheaton: Tyndale House, 1987); *What the Bible Is All About Quick Reference Edition* (Ventura, CA: Regal, 1989). There are also 4 different group study guides for this book.

[5]Another form of this commentary is available solely for the Old Testament and another for the New Testament (Minneapolis: Bethany House Publishers, 1985).

Luther, John Wesley, and other commentators appear at vital doctrinal texts. Because such a variety of commentators are included, the Bethany commentary provides a surprisingly broad spectrum of views. For example, it gives both premillennial and amillennial interpretations of Revelation 20.

Goodwin, Frank J. *A Harmony of the Life of St. Paul.* Ada, MI: Baker Books, 1983.

Goodwin puts the narrative of Paul's life from the Book of Acts in parallel with statements from Paul's epistles, in order to give us a more complete, sequential review of the apostle's life. This book is a practical aid in studying the New Testament, where Paul is such a significant character.

Pentecost, J. Dwight. *A Harmony of the Words and Works of Jesus Christ.* Grand Rapids: Zondervan, 1981.

Dr. Pentecost provides a convenient outline of the major events and teachings from Jesus' life. For each segment of the outline, he reproduces the appropriate passages from all four Gospels, which he quotes from the NIV. This book is a companion volume to his book, *The Words and Works of Jesus Christ*, also published by Zondervan.

Robertson, A.T. *A Harmony of the Gospels.* New York: Harper, 1932.

Robertson places all four Gospel accounts of Jesus' life in parallel columns. This is a time-tested textbook for seminary students, even though Robertson does not provide as much critical apparatus (variants, alternate translations, etc.) as Throckmorton does.

Thomas, Robert L., and Stanley N. Gundry. *A Harmony of the Gospels, New American Standard Version.* San Francisco: Harper San Francisco, 1986.

This Gospel harmony in the NASB is a valuable aid to Christian readers who prefer to use this version. Twelve appendix articles discuss topics such as source criticism, form criticism, and redaction criticism. While the editors take a conservative approach to these matters, their essays are fair-minded and informative.

Throckmorton, Burton H., Jr. *Gospel Parallels: A Synopsis of the First Three Gospels*, 5th ed. Nashville: Thomas Nelson, 1992.

Throckmorton's parallel differs from Robertson's in two important ways: (1) It is based on the NRSV, while Robertson uses the KJV, and (2) it has a detailed critical apparatus to help the serious Bible student, while Robertson's does not.

CHRONOLOGIES

Hoehner, Harold. *Chronological Aspects of the Life of Christ.* Grand Rapids: Zondervan, 1978.

Although calendar dates cannot be assigned to the events of Jesus' life with absolute certainty, Hoehner discusses modern scholars' "best guess" about the date of Jesus' birth, His crucifixion, and other crucial events. He cites interesting quotations from Roman and Jewish histories that help us calculate these dates. It is an engaging discussion, even though not everyone will agree with his conclusions.

House, H. Wayne. *Chronological and Background Charts of the New Testament.* Grand Rapids: Zondervan, 1981.

This "mixed bag" of resources will help you in understanding many areas of New Testament study. Mr. House charts a chronology of Jesus' life, a chronology of Palestine, and a chronology of the Roman Empire. He also illustrates Bible weights and measures, the transmission of the New Testament text, and a variety of other things concerning the New Testament. Pastors and Sunday School teachers will make frequent use of this resource in their teaching.

Walton, John. *Chronological and Background Charts of the Old Testament.* Grand Rapids: Zondervan, 1994.

Walton charts Old Testament events in a conservative manner. He upholds the early date of the Exodus, Jericho's defeat by Joshua, and other points that liberal scholars would debate.

CHARACTER STUDIES

Bruce, F.F. *Paul: Apostle of the Heart Set Free*. Grand Rapids: William B. Eerdmans Publishing Company, 1978.

This character study is Dr. Bruce's best-known work. Bruce draws on his rich knowledge of New Testament culture to give us a vivid portrait of the apostle. Again and again, the author points out Paul's theological genius and fervent personal devotion to Jesus Christ. This book will burn itself into your memory.

Deen, Edith. *All of the Women of the Bible*. San Francisco: Harper San Francisco, 1988.

Only a woman could have written such a sensitive portrayal of Bible women. Mrs. Deen helps us perceive the attitudes and thinking of each woman. This devotional character study is a good resource for group discussion.

Edersheim, Alfred. *The Life and Times of Jesus the Messiah*. Peabody, MA: Hendrickson Publishers, 1993.[6]

Most reviewers agree that this is the best character study of Jesus published to date. Edersheim grasps the deep theological importance of God's incarnation in Christ, and comes as close as one can to expressing it. Some reviewers feel that the abridged edition (entitled simply, *Jesus the Messiah*) is not as good as the original, but it is certainly worth reading.

Packer, J.I., Merrill C. Tenney, and William White. Jr., eds. *All the People and Places of the Bible*. Nashville: Thomas Nelson, 1982.

This compact book is extracted from *Nelson's Illustrated Encyclopedia*. It contains a one-paragraph description of each person and place mentioned in Scripture (excluding the Apocrypha), along with a few key Scripture references. One wishes the information for Apocryphal books had been included; despite that omission, however, the book is a handy reference for teachers and pastors.

---

[6]Also available from (Cleveland: World Publishing, 1990).

Whyte, Alexander. *Bible Characters from the Old and New Testaments*. Grand Rapids: Kregel Publications, 1990.

This work was published as six volumes in 1898-1902. Kregel has done us a great service by reprinting it as one volume, which makes it more convenient and less expensive. Whyte has a colorful way of recreating Bible characters. Though he did not have access to the discoveries of archaeologists in this century, Whyte did have a brilliant imagination and a marvelous gift for narrative writing. This book is a joy to read.

ARCHAEOLOGICAL STUDIES

Barker, Philip. *Techniques of Archaeological Excavation*, third ed. London: B.T. Batsford Ltd., 1993.

If you would like to visit an archaeologists' "dig," this book will take you there. Barker explains step-by-step how the researcher carefully lifts layers of accumulated soil to reveal the treasures of past civilizations. He includes pages from the archaeologists' notebooks, dozens of photos that illustrate each stage of the "dig," and site sketches that reconstruct the original scene. Readers will be entertained as well as trained by this skillfully written book.

Frend, William H.C. *The Archaeology of Early Christianity: A History*. Minneapolis: Fortress Press, 1996.

Professor Frend of Glasgow traces the history of Christian archaeology from the first spadeful turned by Queen Helena (Emperor Constantine's mother) in A.D. 310 to the explosion of new discoveries in the 1990s. Professor Frend writes with a sense of excitement about the field, producing a well-researched orientation text for the serious lay Bible student. At the same time, he narrates the history of archaeological work with warm human interest and humor.

Hoerth, Alfred J. *Archaeology and the Old Testament*. (Ada, MI: Baker Books, 1998).

This long-awaited companion to John McRay's volume on the New Testament also takes a well-reasoned, conservative approach to recent Old Testament discoveries. Hoerth recently retired as director of archaeology at Wheaton College.

Levy, Thomas E., ed. *The Archaeology of Society in the Holy Land.* New York: Facts on File, 1995.

A veritable encyclopedia of archaeology in Palestine, Levy's book features articles by William G. Dever, Nigel Goring-Morris, and 27 other current experts. The book focuses on what archaeology tells us about ancient society, rather than what it tells us about the Bible *per se.* This emphasis makes it a valuable supplemental resource for the serious Bible student. Detailed maps and charts display the information clearly.

McRay, John. *Archaeology and the New Testament* Ada, MI: Baker Books, 1993.

A simply illustrated, clearly written tour of the most important sites of the New Testament world, McRay's book is a good reference for pastors and church-school teachers. McRay teaches New Testament at Wheaton College in Illinois. He does not detour into the exotic theories of some recent researchers.

Shanks, Herschel. *Jerusalem: An Archaeological Biography.* New York: Random House, 1995.

"Through the archaeology of Jerusalem, one can learn about almost everything even remotely connected with the Near East," the author declares (p. xiii). He then narrates this colorful case study to show us how true that is. Shanks' lavishly illustrated book catches the eye with the graphic appeal of a magazine. Well it should, since Shanks is editor of *Biblical Archaeology Review,* the foremost lay-oriented magazine of current archaeology. The book's popular approach does not weaken its scholarly substance, however. Even Bible students who are familiar with the field of archaeology will enjoy Shanks' grand tour of Near Eastern history through the time tunnel of the Holy City.

Stanton, Graham. *"Gospel Truth?": New Light on Jesus and the Gospels.* Valley Forge, PA: Trinity Press International, 1995.

Prof. Stanton describes the most recent Greek New Testament manuscript discoveries and how they help us better understand the ancient world. He illustrates the difficulty that Bible translators face, trying to piece together the faded fragments of decaying scrolls to check the translation of the Bible text. He makes the point that we dare not rely completely on one manuscript or one relic to shape our understanding of Jesus. Rather, we need to view all the pieces together, as a great mosaic. This book gives a helpful perspective on the role of archaeology in Bible translation.

OTHER MISCELLANEOUS

Geisler, Norman L., and William E. Nix. *A General Introduction to the Bible.* Chicago: Moody Press, 1968.

Though the publisher calls this an introduction, it does not fit the pattern of a Bible introduction or a survey. In fact, Geisler and Nix have given us a rather unique book that discusses inspiration, textual transmission, canonicity, and other controversial matters of lower criticism. It is highly recommended as background reading for the serious Bible student.

Meredith, Joel. *Meredith's Big Book of Bible Lists.* Minneapolis: Bethany House Publishers, 1998.

The popularity of secular "book of lists" spurred the publication of several Bible-list volumes in the 1980s. Meredith's was the first and best, originally being released in 1980. The book includes lists of Bible promises, Bible characters, as well as many bits of Bible trivia such as the longest verse in the Bible, the shortest reign in the Bible, etc. Pastors use this book to glean interesting sermon illustrations, while teachers use it to prepare Bible quizzes.

Glossary

ALLEGORY—a story from everyday life that expresses a spiritual or moral lesson. Early Christian Bible commentators tried to interpret each Bible event as an allegory.

ALTERNATE READING—another way of translating or paraphrasing a Bible verse, based on the accepted Hebrew or Greek text. Many study Bibles give these alternates in margin notes or footnotes. *Compare* TEXTUAL VARIANT.

AMILLENNIALISM—the theological view that Christ and His saints will not reign on earth for 1,000 years in connection with His final return.

ANNOTATED BIBLE—a simple type of study Bible with brief introductions and general outlines to the Bible books, and a few notes on significant phrases in the text. *Compare* REFERENCE BIBLE and STUDY BIBLE.

APOCALYPTIC LITERATURE—any prophetic writings concerning the end of the world and/or God's final judgment. Many books of early Jewish and Christian apocalyptic literature were not included in the CANON of the Bible, for various reasons. *See also* ESCHATOLOGY.

APOCRYPHA—a collection of Jewish literature from the intertestamental era (i.e., the time between the writing of the Old and New Testaments). Roman Catholics and some Protestants believe these writings are Holy Scripture.

APOLOGY—a logical defense of the gospel or of any Christian doctrine. A person who makes this kind of apology is called an APOLOGIST.

ARMINIANISM—a theological tradition named for the Dutch theologian Jacobus Arminius (d. 1609), which holds that God gives each person complete freedom to accept or reject salvation. *Compare* CALVINISM; PREDESTINATION.

BIBLICAL CRITICISM—a general term that describes any objective evaluation of the Bible. This may include an evaluation of Bible manuscripts to see how authentic they are (LOWER CRITICISM) or an evaluation of the message they convey (HIGHER CRITICISM).

CALVINISM—a theological tradition begun by John Calvin (d. 1564) and his followers. Calvinism involves PREDESTINATION and several related beliefs—e.g., that man is utterly sinful and unable to save himself; that God is the absolute ruler of the universe and has the sole power to save or condemn individuals; and that all persons should follow the moral tenets of Scripture. *Compare* ARMINIANISM.

CANON—the official collection of books that make up the Bible. The Jewish Council of Jamnia (A.D. 90) formally recognized the traditional list of books that Jews and Christians had accepted as Holy Scripture (the Old Testament), while the Christian community formally recognized the accepted New Testament books at various councils, concluding in the fourth century A.D.

CANON CRITICISM—a method of HIGHER CRITICISM that attempts to trace how the Jewish and Christian communities recognized certain books as divinely inspired Scripture and rejected others.

CENTER-COLUMN NOTE—a note printed between the columns of a two-column Bible page. *Compare* FOOTNOTE and MARGIN NOTE.

CHRONOLOGY—any study of the time sequence of important events. Also, this term may refer to a dated list of Bible events that a scholar develops by studying the Bible's chronology. Some REFERENCE BIBLES give a chronology in their notes.

COMMENTARY—comments on a given piece of literature.

CONSUBSTANTIATION—the doctrine that Christ's body and blood are really present in the communion (Lord's Supper) elements, even though the substance of the bread and wine are not changed. This doctrine, held by Lutherans and certain other Protestant groups, differs from the Roman Catholic doctrine of TRANSUBSTANTIATION.

CRITICAL APPARATUS—a set of textual notes that show the manuscript background and/or TEXTUAL VARIANTS that have a bearing on each passage of Scripture.

CRITICAL EDITION—an edited text of an old book, made by comparing various copies of that book to see which ones seem to best reflect the wording of the original. (*See also* TEXTUAL CRITICISM). The textual critic chooses from each copy the passages that seem most likely to have been in the original book.

CROSS REFERENCE—a reference to a related idea or Scripture passage. Many study Bibles have marginal notes or footnotes alongside every major portion of Scripture, giving the references to other verses on the same theme; these notes are cross references.

CULTUS—a society's religious system and all of the customs, including civil and family customs, stemming from that religion.

DIALECT—a form of a language that departs significantly from the standard language, or from the language as it is recorded in writing. A dialect has its own peculiar vocabulary and expressions that set it apart from the normal language of its day.

DISPENSATIONALISM—a particular view of Bible history which says that although God has but one plan of salvation, He reveals Himself to mankind and deals with mankind in different ways in each successive period (dispensation) of their relationship.

DOCUMENTARY THEORY—a theory of LITERARY CRITICISM developed by K.H. Graf and Julius Wellhausen. They believed that each book of the PENTATEUCH bore the marks of several writers' and editors' work, which could be identified by noting the name of God that each section was apt to use. They and their colleagues eventually noted four editorial sources of the PENTATEUCH: J (Jahwist), E (Elohist), D (Deuteronomic editor), and P (Priestly editor). This is also called the "documentary hypothesis" or the "Graf-Wellhausen hypothesis."

DOXOLOGY—a declaration of praise to God, often in the form of a hymn or prayer.

DYNAMIC EQUIVALENCE—a goal of Bible translating. A translator who strives for dynamic equivalence seeks to express each idea or concept of the Bible manuscripts in modern language, without trying to follow the manuscripts' written pattern phrase-by-phrase or word-by-word. *Compare* FORMAL EQUIVALENCE.

ECLECTIC TEXT—a compilation of passages from various Bible manuscripts that a textual critic may choose as the authentic text of the Bible. In other words, instead of following any single manuscript or CRITICAL EDITION, the critic selects the readings he feels are most authentic.

ENCYCLICAL LETTERS—*See* PATRISTIC LETTERS.

ESCHATOLOGY—the study of things relating to the end of the world, the final judgment, and life beyond the grave. *See also* APOCALYPTIC LITERATURE.

EXEGESIS—a method of Scripture interpretation that attempts to draw the meaning of the text from the meaning of the words themselves. The term comes from a Latin phrase that means "to lead out."

FOOTNOTE—an editor's or translator's note printed at the bottom of a Bible page. *Compare* CENTER-COLUMN NOTE and MARGIN NOTE.

FORM CRITICISM—a method of HIGHER CRITICISM that attempts to discover who wrote a Bible passage and at what time it was written, by identifying the literary genre or form of the writing.

FORMAL EQUIVALENCE—a goal of Bible translating. A translator who strives for formal equivalence seeks to express in modern language exactly what the Bible manuscripts say, phrase-by-phrase or word-by-word. *Compare* DYNAMIC EQUIVALENCE.

FORMER PROPHETS—the books of Joshua, Judges, 1 and 2 Samuel, and 1 and 2 Kings, which are grouped together in Hebrew Bibles because they record the work of Israel's early prophets (before the eighth century B.C.). *Compare* LATTER PROPHETS. *See also* MAJOR PROPHETS; MINOR PROPHETS.

GAZETTEER—an alphabetical list of Bible place names with code numbers keyed to an adjacent set of maps.

GENERAL EPISTLES—the New Testament letters that are not addressed to any specific individual or congregation. These are the letters of James, Peter, John, and Jude. They are also called "Catholic Epistles."

GRAMMAR—a book that introduces you to the vocabulary (list of words), morphology (formation of words), and syntax (patterns of word usage) in a given language.

HAGGADAH—a collection of Jewish anecdotes and folklore, which rabbis use to illustrate the Law.

HALAKAH—a compilation (oral or written) of Jewish Law and the various rulings that rabbis have made, based on the Law.

HERESY—a denial of or a marked departure from the gospel of Jesus Christ. A heretic (one who espouses a heresy) contradicts the Bible's basic teaching about Christ and the salvation He brings. Note that heresy is always HETERODOX, but a HETERODOX teaching is not necessarily heresy.

HETERODOX—being different from the beliefs that Christians have traditionally accepted and taught. *Compare* NEO-ORTHODOX; ORTHODOX.

HISTORICAL BOOKS—books of the Old Testament (Joshua through 2 Chronicles) that are grouped together in Christian Bibles because they describe the history of Israel from the conquest of Canaan to the Babylonian captivity and restoration. Hebrew Bibles refer to these books as the "Former Prophets" (except for Ruth and 1 and 2 Chronicles, which they place in the WRITINGS).

HYPERBOLE—an exaggerated statement made for the sake of vividness or emphasis.

IMPRECATORY PSALMS—psalms that ask God to defeat or destroy the Psalmist's enemies. Some of these, such as Psalms 58 and 137, show strong hatred for the Psalmist's foes.

IMPRIMATUR—a Latin word meaning, "let it be printed." A book must have an *imprimatur* (permission to be printed) from a recognized Roman Catholic official in order for Catholic readers to use it with the Church's approval. However, the imprimatur does not mean that the licensing official agrees with all of the book's contents. *See also* NIHIL OBSTAT.

INCLUSIVE LANGUAGE—an editorial device of using neutral-gender or multiple-gender pronouns, rather than masculine pronouns, to translate Scripture passages that clearly refer to both females and males.

INTRODUCTION—a review of each book of the Bible, usually with an outline of each book, that analyzes various stages of the ongoing relationship between God and man. *Compare* SURVEY.

KOINE GREEK—"common" Greek, the form of the language spoken throughout much of the Mediterranean area after the conquests of Alexander the Great. Koine Greek was the common language of Palestine during Jesus' earthly ministry.

LATTER PROPHETS—the prophetic books of Isaiah, Jeremiah, Ezekiel, and the twelve MINOR PROPHETS, which are grouped together in Hebrew Bibles because they record the work of Israel's later prophets (eighth century B.C. and afterward). *Compare* FORMER PROPHETS. *See also* MAJOR PROPHETS; MINOR PROPHETS.

LECTIO DIVINA (Latin, "divine reading")—the discipline of reading Scripture or other religious literature on a regular basis, prayerfully and with contemplative reflection. St. Benedict of Nursia made *lectio divina* one of the disciplines of the Benedictine monastic order.

LEGEND (map)—the caption for a map that describes the location and the time in history that the map depicts. The legend may also have a scale of measurement, an explanation of map symbols, and other information to help interpret the map.

LITERARY CRITICISM—a method of HIGHER CRITICISM that attempts to discover a Bible writer's identity, the date of the writing, the purpose for writing, etc., by searching for clues in the Bible text itself. A sophisticated type of LITERARY CRITICISM, known as SOURCE CRITICISM, tries to sort out and identify various authors' or editors' work in any given Bible book.

LOWER CRITICISM—the study of old manuscripts in an effort to determine which copies best reflect the wording of the original. Also called "TEXTUAL CRITICISM." *See also* BIBLICAL CRITICISM. *Compare* HIGHER CRITICISM.

MAJOR PROPHETS—the longer prophetic books (Isaiah through Daniel) of the Old Testament, which are grouped together in Christian Bibles. Compare MINOR PROPHETS. *See also* FORMER PROPHETS; LATTER PROPHETS.

MAJORITY TEXT—a collection of the readings given by a majority of all the Bible manuscripts that have been handed down. With a few exceptions, the TEXTUS RECEPTUS is the Majority Text.

MARGIN NOTE—a note printed in the side margin of a Bible page. *Compare* CENTER-COLUMN NOTE; FOOTNOTE.

MASORETIC TEXT—a Hebrew text of the Old Testament that contains vowel signs, breathing marks, and other "pointings" added by late Jewish scribes (Masoretes) to aid in pronunciation. These "pointings" are vital to our under standing of the text, since the early scribes wrote their manuscripts as a continuous stream of letters with no spacing between words.

MIDRASH—expository comments on Jewish Law which were made by scribes during the Exile. *See also* SOFERIM; TARGUMS.

MILLENNIALISM—a particular view of Bible prophecy about Christ's return. Christians who hold this view believe that Christ will reign on earth with His saints for 1,000 years. *See also* AMILLENNIALISM; POSTMILLENIALISM; PREMILLENNIALISM.

MINOR PROPHETS—the twelve shorter prophetic books (Hosea through Malachi) of the Old Testament, which are grouped together in Christian Bibles. *Compare* MAJOR PROPHETS. *See also* FORMER PROPHETS; LATTER PROPHETS.

NEO-ORTHODOX—being in harmony with the beliefs that Christians have traditionally accepted and taught, but reinterpreting those beliefs to fit modern concepts of the nature of God and man. *Compare* HETERODOX; ORTHODOX.

NIHIL OBSTAT—a Latin phrase meaning, "nothing is offensive." It indicates that a book does not contain anything that contradicts or offends Roman Catholic dogma. Normally, a Catholic censor will review a book's contents and decide whether to grant his official approval (the *nihil obstat*). If he does, the book then goes to a higher Catholic official for his IMPRIMATUR. However, neither of these approvals mean that the reviewers agree with all of the book's contents. *See also* IMPRIMATUR.

ORTHODOX—being in harmony with the beliefs that Christians have traditionally accepted and taught. *Compare* HETERODOX; NEO-ORTHODOX.

PARALLELISM—a literary device used by ancient Hebrew poets. Instead of using rhyme or rhythm to match the successive lines of a poem, Hebrew poets used parallel thoughts. That is, they expressed the same idea in different words in each successive line.

PARAPHRASE—the task of rephrasing a piece of literature in the same language. This term also refers to the material that results from such rephrasing. *Compare* TRANSLATION.

PASTORAL EPISTLES—the New Testament letters (1 and 2 Timothy and Titus) that Paul wrote to individual pastors, dealing largely with pastoral concerns.

PATRISTIC LETTERS—letters written by leaders of the Christian church who lived before the time of the Council of Chalcedon (A.D. 451). Some of these letters, called ENCYCLICAL LETTERS, were meant to be circulated to all the churches in that leader's district or province. Many of the patristic letters contain Scripture quotations that help us know what Bible manuscripts the early Christians were using.

PAULINE EPISTLES—the New Testament letters written by the apostle Paul.

PENTATEUCH—the first five books of the Bible (Genesis, Exodus, Leviticus, Numbers, and Deuteronomy). Ancient tradition holds that Moses wrote these five books.

POSTMILLENNIALISM—the theological view that Christ and/or His saints will reign on the earth (or in heaven) before His final return.

PREDESTINATION—the theological view that God chooses some persons to be saved, even before they are born. The less-common doctrine of double predestination further holds that God chooses some people to be damned, even before they are born. *See also* ARMINIANISM; CALVINISM.

PREMILLENNIALISM—the theological view that Christ and His saints will reign on the earth for 1,000 years after His final return.

PROGRESSIVE REVELATION—the gradual process by which God reveals more of His truth to humanity.

REDACTION CRITICISM—a method of LITERARY CRITICISM that attempts to trace how a Bible writer's work has been edited by various scribes and editors (German, *redakteurs*) as it was handed down.

REFERENCE BIBLE—a general term for a Bible with certain study "helps." It may refer to an ANNOTATED BIBLE or a STUDY BIBLE.

SEMITIC—referring to the people who are thought to have descended from Noah's son Shem. In biblical times, the Semites included Babylonians, Assyrians, Arameans, and Phoenicians as well as the Jews. The languages of these peoples were remarkably similar.

SEPTUAGINT—a Greek version of the Old Testament, translated for the Library Alexandria just before 200 B.C. Seventy scholars (from the Greek *septuaginta*, "seventy") are believed to have worked on the project.

SOFERIM—Jewish scribes of the Exile, who copied and interpreted the Scriptures. *See also* MIDRASH; TARGUMS.

SOURCE CRITICISM—a method of LITERARY CRITICISM that attempts to identify various segments of a Scripture passage that originated with different writers or editors.

STUDY BIBLE—a Bible with a fairly elaborate system of study "helps," including detailed introductions and outlines to the Bible books, notes on nearly every verse, a concordance, and other study tools. *Compare* ANNOTATED BIBLE; REFERENCE BIBLE.

SURVEY—a general descriptive review of Bible history which explains how various events revealed more of God's nature and advanced His relationship with mankind. *Compare* INTRODUCTION.

SYNOPTIC PROBLEM—a problem in HIGHER CRITICISM concerning a number of seeming discrepancies in the first three gospels (Matthew, Mark, and Luke). These three books give such similar accounts of Jesus' life that scholars say they are synoptic ("seeing together"). And yet there are differences: events in different sequence, sermons in different order, etc. These differences pose the Synoptic problem.

TARGUMS—Aramaic translations of Jewish Scripture, which were used by Palestinian Jews of Jesus' day.

TEXTUAL CRITICISM—*See* LOWER CRITICISM.

TEXTUAL VARIANT—a different phrasing of a Bible verse, according to another Hebrew or Greek manuscript that the translator felt was not as reliable as his chief textual source. Many study Bibles give these variants in margin notes or footnotes. *Compare* ALTERNATE READING.

TEXTUS RECEPTUS—the "received text," or the text traditionally accepted as being the most authentic text of the Hebrew or Greek Testament.

THEODICY—the doctrine that God is righteous and omnipotent in spite of injustice, disease, and other consequences of evil.

TOPOGRAPHY—the describing and/or picturing of geographic features in a given area. An atlas or geography text are two kinds of topography books.

TRANSLATION—the process of expressing the meaning of a word, a phrase, or an idea in another language. This term also refers to the translated word, phrase, or idea itself. *Compare* PARAPHRASE; TRANSLITERATION.

TRANSLITERATION—expressing the pronunciation of a word in the letters of another language. Also, this term refers to the transliterated word itself. *Compare* TRANSLATION.

TRANSUBSTANTIATION—the Roman Catholic teaching which holds that the underlying "substance" of the bread and wine are transformed into the body and blood of Christ in the ritual of the Eucharist. *Compare* CONSUBSTANTIATION.

TYPOLOGY—the study of Old Testament people, events, or objects as a foreshadowing or "type" of similar people, events, or objects in the New Testament.

UNITARIANISM—a theological tradition that holds that only one God is worshiped by all the people of the earth. Unitarianism denies that Jesus Christ was God in the flesh, and it denies that a person must be saved only through Jesus Christ. Unitarianism also denies that the Holy Spirit exists as a distinct Person of the Godhead.

UNIVERSALISM—the theological view that all people will be saved or all people will be annihilated at death, regardless of their religious experience. Many people who follow the teachings of UNITARIANISM have also embraced the idea of Universalism.

VERSION—a translation of a book into language other than the original. There are versions of the Bible in Latin, German, English, and many other languages (both ancient and modern).

WORD STUDY—a book that explains the meaning of significant Hebrew or Greek words that appear in the Bible. Also, this term refers to any individual's study of a particular Bible word.

WRITINGS—the remaining books of the Old Testament that are not included in the HISTORICAL BOOKS or the PROPHETS, the other major categories of Jewish Scripture. Hebrew Bibles group the Writings together at the end of the Old Testament.

Index